THE
SMART WOMAN'S
GUIDE TO
Interviewing and
Salary Negotiation

Julie Adair King

Chelsea House Publishers
Philadelphia

First published in hardback edition in 1997 by Chelsea House Publishers.

1 3 5 7 9 8 6 4 2

Library of Congress Cataloging-in-Publication Data

King, Julie Adair.
    The smart woman's guide to interviewing and salary negotiation / Julie Adair King
        p. cm.
    Includes index.
    ISBN 0-7910-4437-8 (hardcover)
    1. Vocational guidance for women. 2. Employment interviewing.
3. Wages—Women. 4. Women—Employment. 5. Negotiation in business. I. Title.
HF5382.6.K56 1997   96-34792
650.14'082—dc20   CIP

Acknowledgments

Thanks to all of the career counselors, human resources professionals, recruiters and other experts who so willingly shared their insights and expertise with me. Without your help, this book would not have been possible.

Thanks, also, to Debby Streeter, who provided valuable editorial input, and to Betsy Sheldon, a terrific editor and friend.

Last, but certainly not least, a very special thank you to my parents, Dale and Barbara King, and to my sisters, April Holmes and Rachel Wright, for reviewing my rough manuscript and, more importantly, for providing their continuing love and support.

Contents

Introduction

In a lot of ways, things were a whole lot easier in the old days. If a woman wanted a job, there were no long, stressful interviews to endure. No rigorous questioning about management philosophies, past accomplishments and career goals—in the first place, we weren't supposed to have any, and in the second, no one cared if we did. For the most part, all a career-minded woman had to do was prove she could type so many words per minute and make a decent pot of coffee.

Salary negotiation? That was a man's game, something the big boys did. Society said it was unladylike for women to concern themselves with crass subjects such as money. If a woman did dare ask why she earned half as much as a man doing exactly the same job, she would likely hear that it was because she didn't need as much money. Women just worked for fun and mad money, after all; the man had a family to support.

Well, that was then and this is now—thank heavens! Women today contribute to the work force in fields from medicine to mining, at levels of the corporate ladder that were unthinkable 20 years ago. Thumb through *Working Woman, Executive Female* and other business magazines, and you can find all sorts of encouraging stories about women playing in the big leagues, commanding compensation packages that make the good old boys of the Fortune 500 blanch.

The bad news is that although many things have changed in the working world, many things have not.

Fighting the same old battles

Corporate America is trying hard to accept the idea that women deserve equal status with men in the workplace. But old habits die hard. And in too many businesses, especially in fields traditionally dominated by men, women still do not get a fair shake.

Despite all the various laws that make it a crime, employers continue to discriminate on the basis of gender. Bias against women shows up in job interviews, in recruiting practices and in advancement policies. The laws haven't motivated employers to eliminate wage discrimination, either; according to U.S. Department of Labor statistics, women are paid, on average, 24 percent less than men doing the exact same jobs.

Sometimes, the bias is unconscious. The employer honestly doesn't realize that a particular hiring procedure or management policy is discriminatory. Other times, however, the employer is fully aware that the company's actions are discriminatory and simply doesn't care. From a legal standpoint, such employers have little reason to care. Because of the way discrimination laws are written and the conservative nature of the courts at present, even if a woman does bring a discrimination lawsuit, her chances of winning are extremely, maddeningly slim.

Problems of our own making

Enough to make your blood boil, isn't it? But consider this: We women must shoulder much of the responsibility for our status in the workplace. If we don't get the jobs for which we're well-qualified, if we don't earn the salary we deserve, it's sometimes our own fault.

For reasons explored in Chapter 2, women often don't sell themselves as well in interviews as men do. We don't like to "brag" about past accomplishments. We downplay our successes and are quick to point out our shortcomings.

Many women—especially homemakers entering the work force for the first time or re-entering the job market after raising children—lack confidence in their abilities. They can't convince interviewers they're worth hiring because they don't believe it themselves.

We often hurt our own cause in terms of salaries, too. Again, because of a lack of confidence, we may undervalue our skills and experience. We don't ask for as much money as a similarly qualified man might, and we back down sooner in salary negotiations. No wonder some employers view women as the best bargain around!

Even when it comes to career advancement, we can be our own worst enemies. Many women have the mistaken notion that good work is automatically rewarded. Instead of lobbying for the promotion or raise we've earned, as our male counterparts do, we sit back and wait, hoping our efforts will be recognized.

Of course, not all women suffer from these problems. But even if you're very well-educated, even if you've advanced into the management ranks, there's a good chance that at least some of your career wounds are self-inflicted.

What this book will teach you

If what you've read so far has you feeling a little gloomy, take heart. This book will help you overcome these challenges and more.

The first book in the *Smart Woman* series, *The Smart Woman's Guide to Resumes and Job Hunting*, provides step-by-step advice on how to create an effective resume and also offers a general overview of the entire job-hunting process.

The book you now hold in your hands, as its name implies, takes a closer look at two critical aspects of the job search: interviewing and salary negotiation. For most women, these two areas are especially troublesome, not only because of the way employers view women in the workplace, but also because of the way we view ourselves.

In the chapters to come, you'll learn to:

- Overcome cultural stereotypes that can affect the outcome of your interviews and salary negotiations.
- Sell yourself with confidence to prospective employers.
- Find an employer who truly offers equal opportunities to women.
- Negotiate the salary you deserve, even in a tight marketplace.
- Convince your current employer that you deserve a raise.

You'll learn how to shine in job interviews and how to negotiate the best possible price for your services once the job offer is yours. You'll also discover the secret to negotiating a higher salary in your present job.

Not for women only

Although this book does focus on the special problems that await women in the interviewing and salary negotiation process, it also covers many job-hunting and negotiation pitfalls that have nothing at all to do with gender. Men, as well as women, can benefit from this information.

So if you have brothers, a husband or other male acquaintances in need of a career boost, pass this book along to them. If they're reluctant to accept it because of its title, make a book cover out of last month's *Field and Stream* or some other men's magazine. They'll get the information they need, and no one will be the wiser.

Advice from a broad range of experts

Many aspects of job hunting and negotiation have clear-cut rules. In resume-writing, for example, the experts all agree that a certain length and layout of document makes the most impact on employers. But when it comes to interviews and salary negotiations, things are not so black-and-white. It's not easy to say that any one interviewing or negotiating strategy is best, because so much depends on the situation.

Different employers have different policies about how job applicants are to be interviewed and how much salary negotiation is acceptable.

In addition, the attitudes and personality of the interviewer or person handling the salary negotiations also affect how well a particular strategy will work. Employers try to be objective in hiring decisions, but the subjective opinions of the people involved in making those decisions are always a factor.

It's important that you look at the interviewing and negotiation process from many different viewpoints so that you can determine the best way to proceed in your particular situation. To that end, I've included in this book comments from numerous people who interview job candidates and negotiate salaries every day for a living. Their opinions are representative of what hiring managers, human resources directors, executive recruiters and placement specialists have to say about various interviewing and negotiation strategies.

A look at the chapters to come

Here's a brief preview of what's ahead:

Chapter 1 provides an overview of the types of discrimination women face in interviews, in salary negotiation and in the work force in general.

Chapter 2 explores the flip side of the coin, explaining how traditionally female ways of speaking, acting and thinking can hurt women when they interview for jobs and negotiate salaries.

Chapter 3 discusses the ins and outs of the information interview, an often-overlooked job-hunting tool that can help you define your career goals, lead you to unadvertised job openings and give you an edge on your competition.

Chapters 4 and 5 help you overcome your anxiety about job interviews by taking a realistic look at the process and explaining the different interviewing approaches employers are using today.

Chapter 6 shows you how to use the same techniques that salespeople use to sell their products to market yourself to employers.

Chapters 7, 8 and 9 explore three of the most critical aspects of winning favor with the interviewer: creating chemistry, making a good first impression and communicating your skills with confidence.

Chapters 10 through 15 guide you through the process of preparing for your interview. In Chapters 10 through 14, you learn how to research the company, assess your skills, answer any interview question in a powerful, professional manner and deal with special interview situations, such as out-of-town interviews. You also learn how to interview the interviewer so that you can determine whether the job and the company are really right for you. Then, by completing the role-playing exercise in Chapter 15, you reinforce your newfound skills.

Chapter 16 walks you through important post-interview steps: writing a thank-you letter, assessing your interview performance and evaluating information you obtained from the interviewer.

Chapters 17, 18 and 19 explore the issue at the forefront of most job-seekers' minds: money. Chapters 17 and 18 show you how to negotiate a starting salary with power and finesse. Chapter 19 teaches you how to get more money after you have the job.

Chapter 20 offers a few parting thoughts on dealing with rejection and provides a list of additional resources that can help you with job-hunting and career problems.

There is no quick fix

Unlike some other books on the market, this book does not take the "quick-fix" approach to interviewing or salary negotiation. For example, you won't find scores of canned answers to interview questions or clever statements designed to fool the employer into thinking you're something you're not. Why? Because they don't work.

The only way to persuade employers that you are the best person for the job or that you deserve a certain salary is to convince them that you can solve their specific problems. That means that you must take the time to research the company and the position thoroughly. More importantly, you must take the time to learn about yourself—to assess your unique abilities, skills and experiences and figure out how they will enable you to become the solution that the employer is seeking.

This book leads you step-by-step through the process of learning about the employer, the job and your own qualifications and shows you how to use that information to develop powerful interviewing and salary negotiation strategies. I'll provide you with all of the guidance and assistance I can, but no one can do the necessary research, self-evaluation and preparation but you.

Yes, this approach takes time and effort. But I promise that if you commit yourself to it—if you read all the chapters in this book and complete all of the recommended exercises— you'll gain advantages that far outweigh the cost. You'll not only develop the skills and insights you need to be successful in interviews and negotiations, you'll acquire a level of self-confidence that will automatically make you a more sought-after employee.

Getting ahead in the real world

When the world is a perfect place, all career-minded people, regardless of gender, will have the same opportunity for jobs, salaries and career advancement.

It's not yet a perfect world.

If you go into your interviews, salary negotiation or any other part of the job search denying that disappointing truth, you're hurting your odds of success. You need to be prepared for the biases you may encounter and know how to deal with them. You also need to take a close look in the mirror and determine whether your own behavior is part of what's keeping you down.

As a woman, you still must work harder—and work smarter—than your male counterparts to get the job and the salary you want. This book will show you how to overcome the challenges that await you and find all the success and satisfaction you deserve.

Chapter 1

It's a jungle out there

Imagine that you're walking through a deep, dark jungle. You round a bend and discover that a huge, centuries-old tree has fallen across your path, blocking your progress. What do you do?

Do you stand there kicking and cursing it, hoping that your outrage will convince that tree to move out of your way? Do you sit and wait, confident that someone, someday, will rescue you? Do you throw up your hands and turn back, accepting the fact that for now, you're not meant to go any farther?

The answer, of course, is none of the above. Being the intelligent, rational woman you are, you assess the situation and then figure out a way to either climb over or walk around that tree.

That, in essence, is the same approach a smart woman takes on her career path. By no means should you give up and accept the cultural stereotypes and gender biases that block your progress. Nor should you expect that if you wait patiently enough, some heroic employer will come to your rescue, delivering the job or raise you deserve. It simply won't happen.

On the other hand, kicking and cursing about the unfairness of it all won't do you any good either. Responding to an employer's sexist question or statement with an angry diatribe about women's rights may make you feel better, but it certainly won't win you the job or the pay raise.

Instead, you must take an objective look at the obstacles on the path between you and the salary or job you want. After you understand those obstacles, you can plot out the best way to get around them.

In this chapter, you'll take the first step in the process by examining the major roadblocks you may encounter as a woman in the work force jungle.

The glass ceiling: still shatterproof

A report titled "Good for Business: Making Full Use of the Nation's Human Capital," published by the U.S. Department of Labor in March 1995, documents corporate America's advancements in the area of equal opportunities for women and minorities. Unfortunately, the report holds little good news. Women now make up nearly 50 percent of the nation's work force, but we're still seriously under-represented in upper management. The report estimates that only 3 to 5 percent of senior positions—defined as vice president and above—in private-sector companies are held by women. Of the Fortune 1,000 companies studied in the report, only two had female CEOs.

Many corporate leaders talk up their dedication to equal opportunity, but there's a major difference between what the typical business is saying and what it's actually doing. A big part of the problem seems to be that the average CEO believes that discrimination is a thing of the past—something that used to exist but has been erased by their edicts that all candidates for a job should be given the same consideration. What these company leaders fail to recognize, suggests the Good for Business report, is that the equal-opportunity hiring practices they have demanded are not being faithfully carried out by the middle- and upper-level managers who have the power to make or break an employee's rise up through the ranks.

To many of the white males who comprise the majority of middle- and upper-level management, women and minorities are a threat. As one white male interviewed for the Labor Department report put it: "If (women and minorities) are in, there's less of a chance for me. Why would I want a bigger pool?"

Even among more enlightened male managers—and they do exist—unconscious discrimination can occur. It's simple human nature, say researchers, for a man to prefer a male candidate over a female candidate. Why? Because people tend to hire people who look, act and speak the same way they do— which means that a man is more likely to hire another man than a woman.

This phenomenon is tough to overcome even when employers make it a point to solicit female candidates for executive positions. "The employer thinks, 'We've got all these guys, we'd better hire a female,'" says Susan Rettig-Drufke, whose management-consultant firm specializes in the area of human resources. "But if it's a male doing the interviewing, and he's only worked with men before, his comfort level with a female may not be as high as the comfort level he has with a man. So he may interview a lot of females, but he may not end up hiring any."

Another factor contributing to the glass ceiling is the perception that a woman must be twice as talented as a man to succeed as an executive. "About 90 percent of my clients say they will consider a woman for executive positions. But I know in my heart of hearts they would rather have a man in the job," says executive recruiter Nancy Wright-Nelson. "I always ask, 'Will you just consider a woman, or will you really give her a shot at the job?' They'll usually come back with something like, 'Well...I'll give her a shot at the job, but you understand how difficult this job is, and she's going to have to be some kind of woman.'"

Some employers don't think that any kind of woman has what it takes to be effective in upper management. Although much has been written lately about the trend toward a so-called "female" style of management—in which managers rely on communication skills, empathy for others and team-building to get things done—many employers haven't leapt on the bandwagon yet. They believe that the only valid management style is the traditional male approach, where the boss is king, and threats, loud voices and intimidation are motivational tools.

17

"Time and time again, I've seen women passed over for promotions because employers think women can't make the tough decisions," says career consultant Candiss Rinker. "The common stereotype is, 'Women don't know how to use power appropriately.' The truth is that women wield power differently—they aren't as inclined to be as overtly aggressive and vocal as men. Men misunderstand and misinterpret that style. Because the woman is more soft-spoken, men underestimate her strength and determination."

The lack-of-power stereotype is just one of many stereotypes that a woman faces when interviewing for management positions. The research conducted for the Good for Business report showed that employers also believe the stereotypes that women aren't as committed as men to their careers, are unwilling and unable to work long or unusual hours, are unwilling or unable to relocate, are too emotional, aren't aggressive enough, and are lacking in quantitative skills. And if you happen to be disabled or a member of a particular ethnic group or minority as well as a woman, you have to deal with a whole additional set of negative stereotypes! Even though research has proven that these stereotypes hold absolutely no water, they persist in the minds of employers, helping to keep women and minorities where they are now—at the bottom of the corporate food chain.

As you can see, the attitudes that created the glass ceiling remain very much in play. Even though these attitudes are slowly starting to change, the day when men and women are truly equals in business appears to be a long way off.

Glass doors, glass walls and other traps

As if the glass ceiling weren't enough of a challenge, two other barriers to women's advancement have recently come into the spotlight: the glass door and glass walls.

The term "glass door" is a new label for an old problem: employer reluctance to hire women for jobs that are traditionally considered man's work—construction, manufacturing and the like. If you're a recent college graduate or just a few years into your career, you may be surprised that this problem still exists. After all, you grew up being told that girls can do anything boys can do (and you proved it, too).

The trouble is, a lot of people out there don't think the way you do. Shelley Gates, a gender-equity consultant and former associate director of Women Employed, a Chicago-area organization that offers career-development programs for women and serves as an advocate on women's policy issues, relates an example that illustrates this disappointing truth all too well.

Women Employed recently formed a partnership with an auto-mechanics training program, with the goal of recruiting and training low-income women to enter this male-dominated field. But when the women in the program tried to put their new skills to work, they received a cold reception from prospective employers. "They experienced the same kind of discrimination we saw in the 1970s," says Gates. "When a woman applied for the job, she was given a different job description than a male applicant. All of the sudden the opening wasn't for a mechanic, but for a tire changer or a desk clerk. It was very frustrating and also very shocking to these women, because our society told them that discrimination is gone and you can be whatever you want to be."

Glass walls operate a little differently, but their effect is the same. These invisible barriers also keep women out of certain jobs: in this case, from positions with direct responsibility for producing the company's major products and for generating the majority of the revenue. Such jobs, known as line positions, are the power centers of any business.

The nonprofit research organization Catalyst, in a recent study called "On the Line: Women's Career Advancement," surveyed CEOs and human resources professionals from Fortune 1,000 companies. The results showed that women are steered away from line positions and encouraged instead to work in staff positions—jobs in human resources, public relations, training and other support areas considered "softer" and less critical.

Many companies do name women to the top posts in staff departments. But because their functions aren't as vital to the bottom line of the corporation, staff managers usually don't have as much power (and typically, don't receive as much pay) as line managers.

Don't misunderstand me—becoming director or vice-president of public relations is an excellent career goal, if that's what you dream of becoming. But if you aspire to be the president, CEO or some other major player in a corporation and you think you can make it there from a staff position, you're in trouble. In most companies, employees who move into the highest levels of management come from line, rather than staff, positions.

If you want any chance of breaking the glass ceiling, then, you first have to get past the glass walls and doors.

"So, how old are your children?"

Glass ceilings, glass walls, glass doors—all of this may seem pretty vague to you. The statistics clearly show that gender discrimination is a reality, but how, exactly, does it happen? What are some specific ways that employers treat women differently than men, and how does that unequal treatment affect you? A look at the typical job interview provides some good answers.

First of all, interviewers often ask different questions depending on the gender of the job candidate. For example, nearly all of the employment experts surveyed for this book stated that most employers ask female candidates about their marriage and family status, something they rarely do with male candidates.

The woman on the receiving end of these questions faces a Catch-22: If she refuses to answer, she alienates the interviewer. If, on the other hand, she tells the employer that she has a spouse or family, she's considered a less-desirable candidate for the job. A woman with a family is perceived as someone likely to take time off to have babies, to care for sick children or even to quit to follow her husband on a job relocation.

It's illegal to discriminate on the basis of marital or family status, of course, but many employers are either ignorant of the law or determined to circumvent it. "You have to remember that a lot of interviewers are not human resources personnel who are really up on the law," says Shelley Gates. "They see these questions as just finding out all the ways you might not be able to come to work. They don't see it as discriminatory, and it doesn't occur to them that they never ask men these questions, which is really what makes it illegal."

Many employers who are fully aware of the law simply ignore it. They're smart enough not to come right out and ask whether you're married or have children—doing so might give you cause for a discrimination claim. Instead, they slide the topic into the conversation very subtly. An interviewer might say, "I'm in a bit of a rush today because I'm going to see my boy's school play at Jefferson Elementary. Are any of your children involved in that?"

Interviewers also are more likely to question a woman's dedication to her career. They continue to believe the cultural stereotype that says a woman isn't interested in a long-term job, just in filling her time between babies or bringing in some extra spending money until her husband earns enough to support the lifestyle the family wants. As a consequence, they ask women such questions as, "Why do you want to work?" and "How do you react when things get tough? Do you walk away or stick with it?" more frequently than they do men.

In addition, interviewers tend to relate differently to men than women. Sometimes, male interviewers are downright confrontational with female job candidates. "There are still many diehard chauvinists who believe that women will never compete with men," says Nancy Wright-Nelson. "When they're interviewing a woman for a job they would traditionally have given to a man, they try to break her down. They take her on, dare her to cross a line. I think they're trying to see whether she will back down, hold her ground or fight back if they attack."

Other times, male interviewers are easier on women than on men, says Susan Rettig-Drufke. Which sounds like a good thing, but isn't. "Some men [do this] because they're uncomfortable with women. So they tend to be more condescending or slip into the role of husband or father. This ends up hurting the job candidate because there is an immediate unconscious feeling on the part of the interviewer that this female may not be able to do the job."

Does this mean you're better off when the interviewer is a woman? Not necessarily. "Many women who have succeeded in business have had to buy into the male model of the way things should be. As a result, they sometimes are even firmer enforcers of cultural stereotypes than men," says Dr. Susan Shepherd, acting director of the women's studies program at Indiana University-Purdue University in Indianapolis.

Both female and male interviewers tend to react negatively to women who present themselves as assertively as the typical man, adds Shepherd, who also is an expert in sociolinguistics—the study of how social factors affect the way language is used and interpreted. "People have a certain set of expectations for how women should speak, and those expectations are different from those about male speech," says Shepherd. "If you violate those norms, even though you may be doing exactly the same thing as a male colleague, it's going to be interpreted differently because you're a woman. It's sort of a no-win situation. The woman is likely to be characterized as too aggressive if she uses some of the assertive language tools that are typical of men. On the other hand, if she uses speech patterns more typically associated with women, she may be characterized as too touchy-feely or as not having enough substance."

Okay, let's see: The man gets asked about his latest accomplishments; you get asked about childcare. The man is treated as a fellow professional; you get treated like somebody's daughter or wife. He speaks with confidence and wins the interviewer's respect; you speak with confidence and you're shown the door. Are those glass barriers becoming a little more visible to you?

Seventy-six cents to the dollar

Every so often, a story about the wage gap between male and female workers makes its way into the news. For the past few years, the headline on such stories usually read something like "Women's wages on the rise" or "Good news about women's wages." Take the time to read these stories, and you'll learn that women on average now earn around 76 cents for every dollar earned by men—up about 22 percent from 1979, when women earned 62 cents to the male dollar.

I don't know about you, but to me, a more appropriate headline for these articles would be "Women still lag behind men in wages" or "Women still getting the shaft." Yes, it's great that the wage gap is narrowing, but the fact that women still earn 24 percent less than male co-workers doing the same job is the important story here. The narrowing of the wage gap is even less impressive when you understand that some of the shift stems from a decrease in men's salaries, not an increase in women's pay.

Perhaps it depends on your perspective. If you're old enough to remember the 62-cents-to-the-dollar days, the narrowing of the wage gap probably does seem like wonderful news. On the other hand, if you believe you deserve to earn the same wage as everyone else who's doing the same job, the salary issue is one of the most frustrating aspects of being a working woman today.

To be fair, women have achieved salary equality with men in some fields. In the job category of "mechanics/repairers," in fact, the latest Labor Department report shows women earning slightly more than their male peers. (Of course, as the Women Employed mechanics-training project showed, it's very difficult for a woman to get a job as a mechanic/repairer in the first place.) But in most other fields, being a woman is likely to cost you big bucks.

Women's attitudes toward salaries and salary negotiation are partly to blame. We'll discuss these attitudes in detail in the next chapter, but in a nutshell, the problem is that we're simply willing to work for less. Most women, say the experts who study such issues, ask for less money than men; back down sooner in salary negotiations; and don't ask for raises as often as men. Can you really fault the employers who take advantage of these traits? They're simply negotiating their best deal.

That doesn't mean that employers are completely innocent, however. Many still allow cultural stereotypes and false gender perceptions to affect pay levels. For example, they may offer less money to a 30-year-old woman than they would to a 30-year-old man because they assume she'll drop out of the work force to hop on the Mommy Track after a few years on the job. And believe it or not, some employers still use the rationale that "a man has a family to support" to justify paying lower wages to women. I heard this excuse myself only a few years ago, when I questioned why a male co-worker earned more than I for handling similar responsibilities.

Women also have to combat the long-standing compensation practice that says an employer should only raise a worker's salary by so much in any given year. If you're already paid 24 percent less than a man to begin with, it's hard to achieve pay equity through annual salary increases.

Again, we have a multitude of laws that prohibit employers from paying men and women different salaries for the same jobs. But a lot of employers, says Shelley Gates, have become very savvy about circumventing equal-pay laws. "If they want to pay a man and a woman different salaries for the same sales job, for example, they give the two jobs different titles. Or they give the woman the less advantageous territory. If they really don't want to pay men and women the same, they can find ways to do it."

Justice isn't easy to win

If you find yourself a victim of discrimination, you can always seek justice in the courtroom and sue the employer. Your chances of emerging victorious, however, aren't very good, for several reasons.

First of all, you must provide evidence that your gender was the reason why the employer denied you the job or the same salary and advancement opportunities as a male colleague. To recover damages other than back pay, you must prove that the employer's actions weren't the result of ignorance or an unconscious error, but a clear-cut intent to discriminate. Proving that discrimination occurred at all is difficult because employers can always find some excuse for not giving you equal opportunities—you lacked some skill, you didn't have quite the right employment background, the male candidate was a bit more impressive in the interview. Proving that the discrimination was intentional is even harder. You're not likely to dig up some memo from the company owner that says, "Don't hire women for this job."

Assuming that you can compile enough evidence to substantiate your claim, bringing a lawsuit is a long, expensive road. Before you can even get into court, the Equal Employment

Opportunity Commission (EEOC) must investigate your claims—a process that can take years. According to Maripat Blankenheim, spokesperson for 9to5, a national organization supporting working women, the EEOC is not very well-equipped to handle the enormous volume of claims it must investigate. "The EEOC has been incredibly underfunded, overworked and understaffed for the past 14 years," says Blankenheim, "which has made it difficult for the agency to be very effective. In some regions of the country, there is an enormous backlog of cases pending EEOC action. Women who file pregnancy discrimination suits sometimes find that their children are five or six years old before the suit is resolved."

Compounding the challenges of winning a discrimination lawsuit is the fact that many judges are simply not on the side of the woman. Blankenheim and representatives from other women's-advocacy groups say that the conservative judges who now dominate America's courtrooms tend to favor employers in discrimination suits.

If you do decide to buck the odds and take your employer to court, you'll need deep pockets to pay for a good attorney. The financial burden alone convinces many women to drop the idea of suing, says Blankenheim. "Many women, especially those in low-income jobs, simply can't afford to hire an attorney. The consultation fees alone are beyond their financial reach."

Want some more bad news? Even if you win your case, the amount of your settlement may not be worth your financial and emotional investment. That's because the current laws limit the amount of damages a woman can collect for gender discrimination. The top amount, when intentional discrimination can be proved, is $300,000, and that's only if the employer has more than 500 employees. For employers with 100 or fewer employees, the limit is $50,000.

Because of all these factors, even those organizations who work on behalf of equal rights most often counsel women to think twice before pursuing legal action. You're better off, they say, to ask your employer's human resources department or employee union for help in resolving discrimination complaints. But of course, many employers won't give such complaints the time of day, in which case you have little recourse other than to look for another job.

Forewarned is forearmed

A great majority of the human resources directors I interviewed stressed that their organizations work very hard to eliminate gender discrimination from the workplace, and I believe them. But the evidence remains that in most cases, women still need knuckles of steel to grab the brass ring.

I present this gloomy news to you not to discourage you or to provoke some militant feminist uprising. It's just that it's very important for you to understand the true nature of today's working world. Only by being aware of the kind of gender bias you may encounter can you hope to circumvent it. Forewarned, as they say, is forearmed.

Chapter 2

Is any of this *your* fault?

Chapter 1 spent a lot of time blaming other people for women's problems in the workplace. Now it's time to do a little honest self-evaluation and determine what, if anything, we're doing to hurt our own cause.

As it turns out, we do share some responsibility for our situation. In interviews and in salary negotiations, as well as in everyday job performance, we women tend to speak, act and think in ways that cost us jobs—and money.

"It was nothing, really!"

When we were young, we learned that nice girls were modest, unassuming and patient. We grew up believing that good work brought automatic rewards, that competition wasn't lady-like. These lessons may have served us well in eighth-grade English class, but they kill us in business.

I'm willing to bet, for example, that at some point during your childhood, someone chastised you for crowing about something you did well. Nice girls don't brag, right? Well, it's true that chattering endlessly about your own greatness is not a good thing. But many women take this lesson to such an extreme that they're uncomfortable saying anything good about themselves—which, as you can imagine, puts them at a real disadvantage in job interviews.

Stephanie Whisman, an employment and development specialist at a large agricultural-sales organization, says that although women are starting to get better at interviewing, she notices that many still are reluctant to mention their accomplishments. "They laugh and giggle and get embarrassed when I ask them to talk about something they did particularly well," says Whisman. Countless other employers made similar statements.

According to Dr. Mildred Galloway, a psychotherapist who counsels many career women, even very accomplished women often suffer from this hangup. "They're well-educated and well-prepared for careers, but they don't do very well in interviews because they lack confidence and have problems asserting themselves," she says. "They want so desperately for you to know how great they are, but they feel that they shouldn't brag about themselves."

Such feelings reflect society's attitudes about appropriate behavior for women, says Jane Hassinger, professor of psychology and women's studies at the University of Michigan and a researcher at The Center for the Education of Women. "Women have been taught that it's not good to put themselves in the spotlight, because it might eclipse someone else's turn in the spotlight," explains Hassinger.

When a woman does get up the nerve to tell an interviewer about an accomplishment, she often downplays her success or attributes it to good luck. She'll say, "Oh, that was really no big deal," or "Well, the truth of the matter is that my boss left the department in really good shape, so it was easy to have a good year."

Researcher Cheryl Olson documented this trait in a study she conducted at the University of California-Berkeley in 1989. Olson, who compared the way male and female students responded to typical job interview questions, found that when they answered questions in writing, both men and women attributed their accomplishments to hard work and ability. But when asked the same questions in a face-to-face meeting with an interviewer, the women changed their answers, this time attributing their success to luck. The men continued to claim that they succeeded because of their own effort and ability.

Olson points out that the UC-Berkeley students she studied were a fairly high-powered, intelligent lot. If these women had so much on the ball, why were they hesitant to say so? "I think it's because the face-to-face job interview is both a social interaction and an achievement-oriented situation, and that creates a conflict of roles for a woman," theorizes Olson. In social situations, she explains, women are expected to act self-effacing and modest, while professional situations call for assertive and achievement-oriented behavior.

"It's not that the women don't consider themselves capable or see achievement as something that's wrong for them," says Olson. "But when their social and professional roles are brought into conflict, they have a problem." This hurts women not just in interviews, but on the job as well. "The people who gain the most durable rewards," says Olson, "are the ones who are perceived to be successful because of their efforts or their ability, and not because of luck."

Jane Hassinger puts an interesting twist on the difference between how men and women view their accomplishments: "Research indicates that men tend to overrate the likelihood of their success. So it may be that women's judgment is better— that they're more accurate in how they perceive their successes and abilities. The problem is that this can backfire in an interview. I think what we need to tell women is, 'Your way of assessing your situation is reasonable and humane and often very accurate, but in this particular situation, you may have to lean in another direction to achieve your goal.'"

This one's too hard, this one's too soft

In addition to downplaying their abilities and accomplishments, women often use certain language patterns that damage their credibility with employers, say researchers.

Women tend to use hedges and qualifiers to soften the impact of their words, for example. A woman might say, "They gave me a spot on the board, but it was sort of due to my connections with another sister organization." A man, on the other hand, would simply say, "I earned a spot on the board."

Women also tend to phrase statements as questions, which leaves people with the impression that we're unsure of ourselves. For example, instead of quietly stating, "I think this position deserves $5,000 more in salary," we say something like, "I was sort of hoping to get a little more?"

In the last decade or so, many women have attempted to correct these tendencies by taking assertiveness-training courses. All well and good. But often, in their efforts to be assertive, they sometimes overshoot the mark, going from timid mouse to pit bull. And like it or not, we live in an age in which employers—male and female—are threatened by aggressive women.

A male career specialist who asked to remain anonymous offered this assessment: "When a woman comes across as too aggressive, she'll scare off an awful lot of employers. That behavior might be okay if she were a guy, but she's not."

I know, I know. It's a double-standard, and it's not fair. But until Glenda the Good Witch waves the equality wand over corporate America, that's the way it is, and the smart woman has to be very careful to find that fine line between too soft and too hard. (Later chapters discuss how to do that.)

A blurry business focus

Another common mistake that women make in job interviews and salary negotiations is failing to understand the employer's motivation—which is, in a word, money. Employers aren't interested in giving you a job or a certain salary so that you can be fulfilled or pay your bills. All they care about is how you can boost their profits.

Darla Lane, regional human resources manager for a large financial services organization, observes that women are not as good as men at presenting their accomplishments in a factual, statistical way that appeals to the bottom line. "This can really hinder a woman," says Lane. "You've got to demonstrate what value you add to the organization. That's especially true if you're interviewing with a man. He's really focused on the bottom line because that's generally how he's been brought up in the organization."

Instead of talking about how they can help the company, many women spend their interview time explaining how the job would help them, comments Marianne Ruggiero, vice-president of corporate human resources for J. Crew Group, Inc. "I've interviewed a lot of homemakers who decided that they wanted a career after their children grew up. They walked in the door and had absolutely no understanding about company profitability and how they might contribute to it," says Ruggiero. "They told me that they wanted a job that would be interesting, something that would cover their bills, something that might lead to something else. It was all self-involved."

Like fish out of water

Women who have spent little time in the workplace, whether because they're recent college graduates or homemakers new to the job scene, often don't know how to relate to bosses and interviewers in effective, businesslike ways. Such women often take on the role of daughter or mother instead of business equal.

When I was fresh out of college, I went to work in the instructional television department of the University of Illinois. The department was run by a witty and intelligent man about 20 years my senior. Perhaps because I was on my own for the first time and living five hours away from my family, I often turned to him for advice on personal problems. I bent his ear about everything from roommate squabbles to car troubles.

After about a year on the job, I became terribly frustrated that nobody seemed to take my skills and talents seriously. I felt I was more capable than my work assignments reflected (doesn't everybody?). I wanted a promotion and a raise, and when they weren't forthcoming, I quit to go in search of more challenging opportunities.

It wasn't until years later that it occurred to me that perhaps I had created my own dilemma. If I acted like the naive daughter who needed Dad to solve all her personal problems, why should my boss believe that I could handle more responsibility on the job?

For older women, it's the mothering instinct that often creates problems. They relate to interviewers, bosses and co-workers not as peers, but as children or grandchildren. In interviews, for example, they say things to the interviewer like, "Well, tell me about you, dear" instead of selling their skills. On the job, they spend a lot of time taking care of everyone's personal needs instead of working to advance their own careers. Consequently, co-workers perceive them as great people to head up the company picnic task force, but not to handle important department projects.

Women with families often think about themselves as mothers first and professionals second, if at all—and they tend to present themselves that way in interviews. When asked a question such as "Tell me about yourself," for example, they respond with answers like "I've been married for 10 years to a chemical engineer, and we have two children." It shouldn't come as a surprise that a woman who defines herself in this way to an interviewer is a less attractive candidate than someone who answers, "I offer all the skills and qualities that are necessary to be successful in this job."

"Pardon me, your insecurity is showing."

Many women aren't sure they have anything worthwhile to offer an employer. This is especially true of displaced homemakers, says Stephanie Koons, a recruiter for a national investment-services firm. "About 90 percent of the women I talk to say, 'Gee, I really don't have any skills,'" says Koons. "During the interviewing process, you discover that they really do have many skills—they just don't realize it. You have to convince them that their experience is valuable and marketable."

It's easy to understand why a woman who's spent most of her life as a homemaker—a decidedly undervalued job in modern society—would have a hard time recognizing her own worth in the workplace. But it's not just older women who suffer from a poor perception of their abilities. Jane Hassinger, who as part of her research at the University of Michigan studies the attitudes of college women in their junior and senior years, says she sees this characteristic even among young women graduating today. "One of the most striking things about these women," says Hassinger, "is that they tend to set their aspirations much too low, given their potential."

Why do we think so little of ourselves? Most psychology experts blame the lessons that society teaches us as children. "When a little boy opens his big blue eyes in the bassinet, the world immediately begins to tell him he's got to be strong and independent and make his own way," explains Dr. Galloway. "Culturally, he's supported. Women are born into an environment where they're second-class citizens. And there aren't many role models to teach little girls that women are important and women are worth something."

"Whatever you want to pay me is fine."

Our lack of confidence hurts us in salary negotiations as well as in interviews. Because we undervalue our skills and experience, we tend to settle for less money than our male peers.

Again, that old female upbringing is at the root of the problem, says Galloway. "When women sit across from an interviewer, they get caught in an emotional strait jacket. They're dressed up like big girls but they still have little-girl feelings. They're caught between their grown-up side, which says, 'You're worth more than that!' and their little-girl side, which argues, 'Well, no you're not.' They're willing to settle for less because a big important side of their personality thinks they don't really deserve more."

Women who do attempt to negotiate for more money often shoot themselves in the foot with certain female-oriented behaviors. For example, they tend to talk too much during negotiations. "Women are notorious for being afraid of silence," says Galloway, "so they say something to fill the void. They state their position, and then they restate it. They embroider it, they embellish it, they say it again and again. In the process, they lose all their negotiating power. Capable interviewers interpret this behavior as a lack of confidence. It's a dead clue that they've got the woman where they want her. They know that women are easily intimidated and that they can manipulate that intimidation."

Women also tend to take a "me-oriented" strategy in negotiations. As we discussed earlier, this self-centered approach seldom carries much weight with employers. "Men tell you what they're worth; women tell you what they need," says Darla Lane. "The message from men is, 'I can add value to your organization.' The message from women is, 'I need this much money because I've got these bills to pay.' It sounds much more desperate."

In the same way many of us were taught at an early age to think and talk about ourselves in "female" fashion, many of us learned as children that we should approach money differently, too. Some women still believe that it's unladylike to discuss finances. But more often, women simply place less value on money.

Jane Hassinger reports that in her research, when female college students were asked to rank their top goals in life, money fell about three-quarters of the way down the list, trailing goals such as family, personal dignity, good relationships and community involvement. "It's a value judgment that is then exploited in the workplace," says Hassinger. Women need to toughen themselves to that reality and realize that if they do care about equality, they must push themselves harder in that sphere than they might care to—not because they care so much about money, but because they care about being discriminated against and being undervalued. And money, of course, is the indicator of value in the marketplace."

I'll be the first to tell you that money is not the most important criteria for job satisfaction. My savings account reflects my belief that it's better to earn a pittance for a job you enjoy than to rake in big bucks for work you hate. But if you agree to take less money than your position is really worth on the open market, you not only hurt yourself financially, but emotionally.

"Usually, women who settle for less than the job is worth are secretly angry and resentful that they weren't offered more," says Galloway. "They don't realize that in the workplace, you don't get what you deserve, you get what you negotiate."

Patient little soldiers

When it comes to moving up the corporate ladder, the glass ceiling isn't all that impedes women's progress. Again, lessons we learned in childhood—combined with our own ignorance

34

about how the working world operates—make our path even more difficult.

For example, says Galloway, many women learn in childhood that good work will automatically bring the rewards it deserves. "They discovered early on that they got attention from others when they did well in school. When they worked even harder, they got more attention. And so they got locked into this pattern of behavior called the 'Good Student model.'"

The problem is that in the workplace, hard work doesn't always get noticed, let alone rewarded. But instead of letting their employers know what they've accomplished, as their male counterparts do, women decide that the way to get the recognition or raise they deserve is to accomplish more. "They ratchet up their behavior and work even harder," says Galloway. "They think, 'I'll do even more and then I'll get rewarded.' But they defeat themselves because employers love this kind of employee. Who wouldn't? They're compliant and nonconfrontational."

In contrast, says Galloway, male workers ask for rewards and recognition for their work. "They give out a certain amount of effort and in turn, they ask for equivalent compensation. And if they don't get it, they're gone."

Darla Lane observes the same patterns in the men and women in her company, noting that the people who get the promotions are the people who ask for them. "In general, women wait to be asked to step into a position because they have done good work," she says. "With men, advancement is more of an expectation. They say, 'If I do this, I'm going to get the promotion, and I'm going to tell you when you're going to give it to me.' I think women need to be a little more aggressive in that regard."

A lot of women, adds Galloway, expect everything in the workplace to be fair and equitable, just the way they learned the world should be in Sunday school. So they're outraged when the squeaky wheel gets the promotion or when someone gets a job because of networking connections. "These women want to play fair and expect everyone else to play fair," says Galloway, "but what they fail to realize is that playing fair simply means playing by the rules. And every game has different rules. If you're playing Monopoly, you don't use the rules for

Scrabble. If you're going to play the business game, you've got to know what the rules are."

What we do right

Now that you've heard about all the female traits that hold women back, it's time for some good news. Although women come in second to men in some aspects of interviewing and salary negotiation, they outperform them in others.

What things do women do better than men? They're more enthusiastic, for one thing. "The majority of women I interview are more enthusiastic and energetic," says Stephanie Whisman. "The men try to be too macho and laid back, and that's not an attitude I'm looking for in potential employees." This is an important plus for women: Employers cite enthusiasm as one of the top qualities they seek in job candidates.

Employment experts also notice that women often are better than men at establishing rapport with interviewers. "Women are more effective in setting a comfortable climate," says Marianne Ruggiero. "They're also better at assessing the climate throughout the interview and adjusting to it." This, too, is a major advantage, because personal chemistry is considered a key to success in the job interview and in the workplace.

In addition, the business world is finally beginning to value so-called "female characteristics"—such as empathy for others, a team-based approach to management, listening skills and emotional awareness. As I said in Chapter 1, this philosophy hasn't been wholeheartedly embraced in many companies, but most business analysts say that it will gain further acceptance as years go by.

Finding the balance

As a working woman today, you hear many conflicting messages. On one hand, you need to banish all of those female behaviors that are holding you back. On the other hand, you need to hang on to those behaviors that employers perceive as positive. You're supposed to be more like a man in some ways and just the opposite in others. The only thing that's crystal-clear is that this is a very confusing time to be a working woman.

In the rest of this book, we'll take an even closer look at how your female upbringing might be affecting you in interviews and on the job. We'll examine specific interviewing and negotiation tactics so you can find just the right balance between shy, unassuming mouse and overzealous attack dog. You'll learn to present yourself with confidence and to become a smart negotiator—without losing those female characteristics that employers are starting to seek out today.

Of course, some of the mistakes you might make during interviews and salary negotiations have nothing at all to do with gender. They're common errors made by men and women alike. You'll learn how to avoid these problem spots as well.

Okay, enough theory and introduction. We've taken a broad look at the challenges you face as a woman in the work force; now, on to the solutions.

Chapter 3

The information interview

In the next chapter, you'll begin acquiring skills and information that will help you shine in job interviews. But first, you need to learn about another type of interview: the information interview.

The information interview is one of the most valuable job-hunting tools available to you. It helps you find out which companies are hiring, what jobs are available, what skills those jobs require and whom to ask for job interviews. In other words, it gives you a head start on the competition.

Oddly enough, most job-seekers don't take advantage of this opportunity. Others abuse it, doing themselves more harm than good. In this chapter, you'll discover why the information interview is such a vital part of a successful job search, and you'll learn the right way to arrange and conduct these important meetings.

What it is and what it isn't

The first thing you need to know about an information interview is that it is not a job interview. Rather, it's your chance to get the information you need in order to find a job that's really right for you.

Here's how it works: First, you do some research to find companies that might be a good match for your skills and interests. When you locate a potential employer, you contact someone who works for the firm and arrange a brief meeting. During this meeting, you gather information about careers or jobs that interest you, asking your contact about such topics as:

- Pluses and minuses of the job/career.
- Qualifications you need to succeed.
- Salary potential.
- The current and future employment outlook.

In addition to learning about possible career options, you find out more about the employer, by asking questions such as the following:

- What aspects of the business are working well?
- What problems need to be solved?
- Can you describe the corporate culture here? (Corporate culture refers to the day-to-day work environment, management philosophies, attitudes toward women, and so forth.)
- Is your company currently hiring people, and do you know of any other companies in the industry that might be looking for help?
- Who are the best people to contact about specific job openings?

This information-gathering process helps you determine whether the career moves you're considering are good ones. You also get the inside scoop on what jobs are available and who's responsible for hiring people to fill those jobs. Perhaps most important, you get a foot in the employer's door—which, as you're about to learn, puts you on the fast track to a new job.

Get the personal edge

One of the biggest benefits of conducting an information interview is that you establish a personal relationship with the employer. To understand why this is so important, you need to understand how most jobs are filled today.

Suppose a job opens up in the accounting department at Hannon Publishing Company, and it's the responsibility of Kristen Matthews, the department manager, to fill the position. The first thing Kristen does is ask her staff whether they know anyone who would be good for the position. She then asks the same question of her other professional and personal contacts—her friends in the city accounting society, her neighbors and her tennis league pals.

After a week or two of this networking, Kristen has the names and resumes of five qualified candidates. From this small pool of talent, she selects her new employee. The job opening is never advertised in the classifieds, listed with a search firm or otherwise announced to the public.

Why do employers prefer this method of hiring? Because they think that a candidate recommended by an employee or professional associate is a better risk than a total stranger. The "who-do-you-know" system also is cheaper than using search firms, classified ads and other traditional recruiting methods.

What all of this means to you, obviously, is that you have a much better shot at a job if you know somebody who knows the employer. And conducting information interviews is one way to get to know a lot of somebodies.

Becoming the answer to their prayers

Information interviews also give you insights you need to shine during your job interviews. For example, imagine that you're investigating job opportunities in the field of corporate communications, and you conduct an information interview at Harris Hardware Corporation. During the information interview, you learn that the corporate communications department has a morale problem; employees are angry at upper management because of recent department restructuring.

Two months later, the department manager is fired, and you're invited to interview for the job. If you hadn't conducted an information interview, you might not be aware of the department's sinking morale, and you might spend most of your interview time selling your superior editing and writing skills. Because you are clued into the situation, though, you know to focus instead on your team-building skills. You take a giant step toward convincing the interviewer that you're the answer to the department's problems.

Finding a job that fits

Another benefit of information interviews is that they help you locate an employer whose corporate culture suits your nature and your needs. During your information interview, you can find out whether the company's work environment is formal or relaxed, for example. You can find out whether everyone must adhere to a strict, 9-to-5 schedule or whether flextime is a possibility. If you're a woman with a desire to work your way up to a senior-level position, you can find out whether women in the company have a chance of advancing or whether the sign on the door to the executive suite clearly says, "No women allowed."

You're going to be spending a lot of time at work, and if the corporate fit isn't right, you're not going to be happy. Nor are you likely to be very successful at your job. Which means that before too long, you'll be job hunting again. So do yourself a favor: Invest the time up front in information interviews and find a place where you can thrive and enjoy your working hours.

Step 1: Think about what you want

Let's look closer now at the specifics of conducting an information interview. Your first task is to determine your immediate and long-term job goals.

When you ask someone for an information interview, one of the first things that person will say is, "What kind of work are you interested in?" If you don't have an answer to that question, you make it hard for your contacts to help you. In order to steer you in the right direction, they need at least some idea of your destination.

You don't have to come up with anything as detailed as "senior marketing manager of laboratory equipment at a mid-sized medical-manufacturing corporation." You do, however, need a general career objective—"a management-level job in marketing," for example.

You say you don't know what you want to be when you grow up yet? That's okay; determining which career is best for you is part of what you're trying to accomplish during your information interviews. But have at least two or three career possibilities in mind. In answer to the "What are you looking for?" question, you might say something like:

"I'm really open to exploring any options at this point. But with my skills, background and interests, there are three areas in which I think I'd be successful: sales, marketing and public relations."

This information helps your contacts help you. They now can start thinking about how you might fit into their company, what jobs are open in those fields and who might have other job leads for you. Being able to state your goals also shows that you're serious about your career and that you're a well-focused individual—traits employers value highly.

Step 2: Develop a list of possible contacts

After you determine your general career goals, it's research time. You need to locate the people who can give you more information about how to reach those goals. To find these contacts, read business magazines and newspapers, review annual reports (check your public library or call companies directly), and most importantly, talk with your friends, relatives and professional acquaintances.

The ideal information interview contacts, of course, are people responsible for hiring in your field. In most cases, these people are not in the human resources department. Although HR specialists play an important role in the hiring process, it's usually the department manager or supervisor who makes the final hiring decision. If you're interested in a marketing position, for example, try to arrange information interviews with marketing managers or directors.

At this stage of the game, though, virtually anyone who works for a company that employs people in your field is a good place to start. The guy who manages the art department may not know whether there are opportunities for you in the marketing department, but he probably can introduce you to somebody who does. You can then ask that person for the information interview.

Step 3: Ask for the interview

Now comes the part that's uncomfortable for many people: asking for the information interview. Women seem to be especially reluctant to do this—they feel as though they're imposing on someone's time. If you're nervous about asking for the interview, think about how you'd feel if the shoe were on the other foot. You'd probably be happy to help. In fact, you'd probably be flattered that someone asked you for advice. Most people you call will feel the same way.

When you ask for the interview, begin by giving the name of the mutual acquaintance who referred you. This is not to say that you can't cold-call complete strangers, too—it's just that your odds of success are better if you have a name to drop. People are more receptive to helping friends of friends.

After you introduce yourself, explain why you're calling. You might say something like this:

> *"I'm thinking about making a career move, and [our mutual contact] said you would be a good person to ask for advice. I was hoping we could get together for a short meeting sometime soon. I'd like to pick your brain about the marketing field in general and also about whether you think it would be a good idea for me to pursue opportunities at your company."*

Stress that you're not asking for a job interview, just for some information and guidance. If the contact says yes to a meeting, establish a convenient time, date and place for the interview. (Offering to buy lunch is always a nice touch.) If, however, the contact is unable or unwilling to meet you, ask for the name of someone else in the company who might be agreeable to doing so.

After you hang up the phone, you have two quick letters to write. First, send a short note to thank the contact for agreeing to talk with you. Restate the date and time of the information interview and say that you're looking forward to your meeting. Second, write a note of thanks to the person who put you in touch with that contact.

Step 4: Prepare yourself

Before the interview, spend a bit more time researching the company so that you can ask intelligent questions. Learn all you can about its products, its competition, its standing in the marketplace and its future plans.

Next, make a list of the questions you want to ask during the interview, remembering that your goals are two-fold. First, you want to find out more about the career path you're considering. Then, you want to learn more about the company itself.

Your list should include questions such as:

- What skills and experience do I need to be successful in the jobs I'm considering?
- What are the pluses and minuses of working in this field?
- What's the marketplace like for people with my level of experience?
- Can you give me a general idea of the salary range for this type of job?
- How would you describe the corporate culture at this company?
- What do you like and dislike about working here?
- What is the company's management philosophy?
- Is the company planning any future expansion?
- What are some of the problems you deal with on a day-to-day basis?

Step 5: Conduct the interview

On the day of the interview, arrive on time, dressed in your professional best. Even though this isn't a job interview, you and your contact both know that a job is your ultimate goal. Conduct yourself accordingly.

As you gather information, step lightly. Don't say anything you wouldn't say during a real job interview. For example, although it's okay to ask about the department head's management style, it's not okay to say, "I've heard through the grapevine that your boss is a real idiot. Is that true?" In the same vein, resist the temptation to divulge any dirty little secrets about your current employer or your personal life. Keep everything on an ultra-professional level.

In addition, never turn the meeting into a sales call, trying to convince the contact to hire you. If you do, you lose all credibility; you said you only wanted information, not a job interview. You shouldn't even offer a resume at this point unless the contact expressly requests one.

Pay attention to the clock and don't overstay your welcome. When your scheduled time is up, thank the contact and ask for the names of other people you might call for information about opportunities in your field.

The evening after your interview or the next day at the latest, write a brief thank you letter to the contact. If the subject didn't come up during the interview, you can take this opportunity to forward your resume:

> *"I've taken the liberty of enclosing a copy of my current resume. If you happen to encounter anyone who might need someone with my skills, I would be grateful if you would let me know. You can reach me at..."*

"Really? You have an opening?"

If you go on enough information interviews, odds are good that you'll stumble across a real, live job opening along the way. During your information interview with the sales manager of Holmes Electronics, for example, you might learn that the Eastern region account executive turned in his resignation that morning. (Okay, so maybe that kind of gem won't be dumped in your lap very often, but it can happen.)

If you find yourself in this fortunate situation, keep your cool. Express your interest in the job and ask to arrange a second meeting at a later date to talk more about the position. But keep the focus of the present meeting on information gathering.

Of course, if the sales manager wants to discuss the position immediately, by all means take advantage of the opportunity. You have to play these situations by ear, letting the contact set the tone. But, as mentioned earlier, you'll lose your credibility (and annoy your contact) if you push to turn the information interview into a job interview.

Time well spent

Conducting information interviews may seem like a lot of work to you—and it is. But if you want to find a position that you'll truly enjoy instead of "just another job," information interviews are more than worth the time and effort. Think of information interviews as window-shopping trips: You're cruising the employment mall to find out what type of jobs fit you best and what employers offer the kind of environment and rewards you want.

Information interviews also give you a chance to acquire essential industry data and polish the communication skills you need to be successful in job interviews. Every minute you spend in information interviews provides you with insights and experience that not only help you locate the perfect job, but also help you convince the employer to give it to you.

Chapter 4

Taming your interview fears

If you're like most people, the prospect of a job interview provokes as much stress and anxiety as a blind date...or a visit from your mother-in-law...or whatever other terror haunts your nightmares.

Oh sure, you feel terrific when they first call you about the interview. Somebody wants you! This could be your ticket out of a job you hate! Your financial problems are solved! You can tell your boss to take this job and—it's going to be great!

But then, the warning sirens go off. And all the little soldiers from your Legion of Self-Doubt leap to action. They tramp through your head, stomping out your excitement, frantically alerting you to all sorts of terrible possibilities. What if you say the wrong thing? What if they ask you about that big blunder you made way back when? What if you get so nervous that you start to giggle uncontrollably, or worse, let out a big snort when you laugh at the interviewer's joke? One little misstep, and poof! There goes your shot at the one really great job left on this planet.

In seconds, you go from euphoria to panic. In a few seconds more, you convince yourself that you're doomed to interview failure.

The danger of this sort of response—aside from losing a few nights' sleep or gaining five pounds (from gulping rocky-road ice cream to relieve your stress)—is that it usually creates a self-fulfilling prophecy. Walk into your interview believing that you're going to fall on your face, and you'll undoubtedly find a way to do so.

It's normal to be a little anxious about your job interviews. But if you let your nerves get out of control, you'll never be able to create a professional, well-spoken image during your interviews, let alone come up with good answers to interview questions.

The first secret to interview success, then, is to learn to tame your fears. And the secret to doing that is to get a better understanding of the interviewing process, which you'll begin to do in this chapter. When you know what to expect, the job interview isn't nearly so frightening.

It's a two-way street

Most people view the interview from a one-way perspective. They see the interviewer as the one with all the power. This is natural, of course, because the interviewer does have the power to give you something you want—the job. Remember, though, that you have something the interviewer finds attractive, too, or you wouldn't be in the interview in the first place.

Don't picture the interview as an interrogation, with the employer acting as the prosecuting attorney and you playing the role of helpless suspect. Instead, think of it as a two-way interaction during which you and the employer determine whether you meet each other's needs.

Some job-hunters are reluctant to ask questions about the job or company during interviews because they're afraid that they'll offend the interviewer. But in fact, employers consider it a negative if you don't ask such questions.

Companies invest a lot of money in hiring and training employees, so they want you to be sure that the job is to your liking before you sign on. They know that if something about the corporate culture or the job itself goes against your grain, you'll either be unproductive or quit after a short time. For that reason, most employers don't approach the interview from the viewpoint of, "We ask the questions here, buddy." They see it as a mutual give-and-take, where each side does some asking and each side does some answering.

When you start getting that nervous, "Will they like me?" feeling, remind yourself that the interview is just as much your chance to interview the company as it is their chance to interview you.

They're probably nervous, too

In large companies with well-established human resources departments (commonly referred to as "HR"), your first interview might be with a member of the HR staff. Because they're trained and experienced in the art of interviewing, HR people generally are calm and collected during the question-and-answer process. You might feel like a nervous kitten in comparison. Fortunately for you, HR people also are trained in the art of putting interviewees at ease.

If, however, your interview is with someone who doesn't have a human resources background—a department supervisor, for example, or the owner of a small business—things are very different. Often, such interviewers don't really know what they're doing. They may have very little or no experience in questioning or evaluating potential employees. Interviewers who lack this experience usually are as uncomfortable and nervous as you are—and just as likely to commit some interview faux pas.

Certainly this was true in my experience. During the years I spent as an associate magazine editor, I was called upon to interview editorial assistants. Having only a vague idea of what I was supposed to do during these interviews, I picked out a few questions from one of those "9,000 Tough Interview Questions" books. But I felt really stupid asking them, and I'm sure my discomfort was apparent. I was so grateful to the one candidate who was able to turn the interview into a semi-normal conversation that I recommended her on the spot, even though I had reservations about her qualifications.

Years later, Helen O'Guinn, the woman who was my boss at the time, admitted that she'd had the same sort of difficulties early in her career. Whereas I relied on those tired old questions about 10-year career goals and such, she took another approach: She didn't ask any questions at all. "I'm much better at interviewing now," says O'Guinn, "but it used to be that when I'd interview people, I'd bring them into my office, tell them what the job entailed and then ask them if they had any questions. And that was the end of the interview. After they left, my boss would ask me how I liked the different candidates. My response was, 'Heck, I don't know, I didn't find out anything about them.' I think that's a real tendency among people who haven't done much interviewing."

In later chapters, you'll learn how to deal effectively with interviewers who don't have much experience at the game. For now, just keep in mind that when you shake hands with an interviewer, you probably won't be the only one with sweaty palms.

It's not the only good job on the planet

However much you may want this particular job, it's not the only opportunity out there for you. If you're smart about the way you go fishing for jobs, you'll discover a lot of great catches in the employer pond.

I'm not saying that you shouldn't take every interview seriously, just that you shouldn't approach it as a life-or-death situation. If you do, you'll only make yourself 10 times more nervous than you need be—which, of course, makes you more likely to fail at what you're trying so desperately to accomplish.

Furthermore, if they don't pick you over the other candidates for the job, it doesn't mean that you're worthless or undesirable or a major career reject. It simply means that someone else's skills and experience more closely matched the employer's needs. Move on to the next prospect and use all of the experience you gained in this interview to make your next one better.

Focus on more important issues

The final key to calming your interview nerves is preparation. If you take time before the interview to reflect upon your skills and accomplishments and to adequately research the employer and the position, you'll be ready for anything the interviewer throws at you. Just as studying helped you feel more confident about taking tests in high school, proper interview preparation helps you be more sure of yourself when you meet your prospective employers.

In this chapter, you took the first step in the interview-preparation process by taking a clear-headed look at the nature of the beast. In chapters to come, you'll learn which skills and qualities are most important to employers, and you'll discover the most effective ways to sell yourself in interviews. Finally, you'll develop and practice your interview "sales pitch" until it feels natural to you. By the time the big day rolls around, you'll be so well-prepared you'll surprise even yourself with your confident—and relaxed—interview performance.

Chapter 5

Interviewing styles and trends

It probably comes as no surprise to you that the job market today is more competitive than ever. No doubt you've heard all the statistics about the ever-increasing numbers of people competing for a diminishing number of jobs.

What may be surprising to you, however, is that even with a very crowded marketplace, employers say they still have trouble finding "good people." This sentiment was repeated to me time after time by human resources personnel and hiring managers, both by those recruiting senior-level executives and those responsible for entry-level hiring.

Just what do they mean by "good people?" In general terms, people who stay on the job long enough and are productive enough for the company to realize a profit from its investment in them.

It costs a lot of money to recruit, hire and train new employees. When a new hire doesn't work out, the employer loses a substantial chunk of change. This has always been a problem, of course, but in today's lean times, with companies searching every office cubicle for ways to trim costs, reducing the number of bad hires is a critical issue.

As a result, employers are adopting or experimenting with new approaches to interviewing. If you're expecting a traditional interview, where the employer asks you a list of rote questions such as "Where do you want to be in five years?", you may be very surprised on interview day. Although the old-school interviewing approach is still in use, especially among untrained or inexperienced interviewers, the trend today is toward more sophisticated interviewing techniques. This is especially true in large companies that have well-established HR departments.

It's important that you learn to recognize and adapt to the different interview philosophies in vogue today. You also should realize that despite the different interviewing tactics they may use, all employers are searching for the same qualities in prospective employees. In this chapter, we'll look at the basic interview styles you may encounter and explore the qualities that make you an attractive job candidate no matter what interviewing approach the employer prefers.

No more easy answers

In the past, many books on interviewing presented a list of the most popular interview questions and then suggested generic, "safe" answers to those questions. A lot of job-seekers—and employers—used these books as interviewing bibles. Employers memorized the questions; job-seekers memorized the answers. Pretty soon, everyone was giving the same answers to the same questions. And each side left the interview knowing nothing about the other except that they had read the same books.

Although you'll still run into interviewers who rely on from-the-books questions, many employers consider them a waste of time. They say that when they ask those questions, all they get are prefab responses that don't provide any insights into the candidate's personality or ability.

What are employers asking today? The focus now is on behavioral interviewing, says David Kornhauser, who manages the HR department at Northwestern University. "The behavioral interview is based on the premise that the best predictor of future behavior is past behavior. So when you ask applicants questions, you ask for specific behavioral examples." Instead of asking "What are your biggest weaknesses?" for instance, the behavioral interviewer might ask, "Tell me about the biggest mistakes you've made on the job and how you rectified those mistakes."

From the examples you provide, employers determine whether a particular problem—or area of success—is a recurrent theme in your work history. Employers look for patterns of behavior and common responses to problems and work situations, realizing that you're not likely to change dramatically when you come to their company.

The conversational interview

Interviewers today also tend to prefer a more conversational style of interviewing. Instead of a question-and-answer volleyball game, the interview becomes more like a professional discussion, with each side contributing equal amounts.

This style of interviewing often throws off people who are used to the more traditional, one-sided interview, says Marilou Clark, who spent many years as a corporate recruiter and HR specialist before starting her own personnel consulting firm. "Women," comments Clark, "were better able to relate to me on a conversational basis. Men who had been around for awhile were sometimes uncomfortable because they expected to play by certain rules that I didn't follow."

The reason interviewers like the conversational style of interviewing is the same reason they're turning to behavioral interview questions. It allows them to get more candid information from the applicant. People are simply more likely to be honest and forthcoming during a relaxed discussion than they are during an interrogation.

As the interviewee, you must be aware of this potentially deadly trap. You need to do your part to foster the conversational tone that interviewers prefer, but you must never get so relaxed that you start spilling your deep, dark secrets or begin relating to the interviewer in an unprofessional manner. Be friendly, but keep your guard up.

The HR factor

For many years now, career experts have advised job-seekers to avoid the human resources department (formerly known as the personnel department) like the plague. HR, so the thinking goes, exists only to eliminate the majority of job-seekers from further consideration. Far better to bypass HR and go straight to the person in charge of the department in which you want to work (a.k.a. the hiring manager) to inquire about job openings.

Author and career-publication editor Betsy Sheldon and I advocated this approach in our first book, *The Smart Woman's Guide to Resumes and Job Hunting.* We still believe it to be the best way to get a jump on the competition. In most cases, the hiring manager knows about the job opening first and ultimately decides whether or not you win the job.

However, if the company does have a human resources department, your first job interview is likely to be with someone from that department, not with the hiring manager. It's important not to behave as though the interview with HR is less important than interviews with department supervisors or managers.

HR departments are much more sophisticated than personnel departments of old, and the role they play in the interviewing and hiring process is becoming increasingly more important. In many companies, the HR interviewer's evaluation of you often carries as much weight as that of the hiring manager. So don't let all the stuff you hear about bypassing the personnel department fool you into thinking you can take the HR interview lightly. If you don't pass this first-round test, you don't move on to round two.

The team approach

In an effort to get a better fix on job candidates, many companies ask a whole slew of people to participate in the interview and evaluation process. Depending upon the level of job you're seeking, you may interview with an HR specialist, the hiring manager, the hiring manager's boss and even staff members who would be your peers. In small companies, you may have to sell yourself to the entire staff.

This team approach to interviewing is referred to as consensus interviewing. It means that many different people interview you and then get together to debate whether they like you well enough to hire you. Sometimes, each person on the interview team asks a different slate of questions. Other times, they all ask the same thing. This can happen by design, if the company wants to see whether you change your answers along the way. Or it can happen by accident, when the interviewing team doesn't work together to plan out any particular interview strategy.

In later chapters, you'll learn some techniques that will help you win over the entire interviewing team. In the meantime, if the concept of facing a long line of interviewers frightens you, think of it this way: The more people you talk to, the more chances you have to sell yourself and to learn whether the company is a good fit for you.

Testing, testing . . .

Because assessing a candidate's strengths on the basis of a resume and interview alone can be difficult, many employers require applicants to take certain employment tests. One such test is the psychological profile or personality test, which aims to determine whether your yin and yang matches the company's yin and yang. In a 1994 Northwestern University study of employers across the country, 22 percent of those surveyed said they use psychological testing to evaluate job candidates. Sometimes, candidates must interview with a psychologist as well as complete a personality profile test; 6 percent of the employers surveyed in the Northwestern study said they require candidates for certain positions to interview with a psychologist.

According to Northwestern's David Kornhauser, the use of psychological screening is on the upswing. "These things go through cycles," says Kornhauser. "We saw a definite decline in the use of personality tests during the Civil Rights era, but now they're coming back into vogue, particularly at the senior level."

In addition to having your psyche evaluated, you may have to perform a variety of skills tests. Employers have long required applicants for secretarial jobs to take typing tests; now, they're also requiring candidates for many other types of positions to pass aptitude or skills tests. Candidates are sometimes asked to deliver a mock sales presentation, edit a written document, use a particular computer program or otherwise prove their knowledge and ability.

What's the likelihood that your interview will incorporate these elements? That depends on the employer and the type of position. You may have to pass muster with only one interviewer, or you may have to pass a series of psychological and technical exams. The smart applicant, however, prepares for any interview possibility. (More on how to deal with personality profile tests, psychological interviews and other employment tests in Chapter 14.)

Computer interviews

If you're a regular reader of your newspaper's business section, you've probably come across articles about the use of computers in the hiring process. Just as computers have become a part of every other aspect of modern business, they're now being used to screen and evaluate job applicants. Some companies are posting job openings over online services such as CompuServe, while others are using special software programs to screen resumes. And some companies are even using computers to conduct interviews. That's right—instead of talking with a real-live human being, you interact with a computer, responding to a series of questions by touching the computer screen or tapping out answers on a keyboard.

Fortunately for the technology-shy, these Jetsons-like scenarios are the exception rather than the rule. Although more and more employers will probably advertise openings on-line and take advantage of resume-screening software in the future—both options are potential time- and money-savers— few companies are taking advantage of them today. And it's very unlikely that you'll be interviewed by a computer anytime soon. Why? Because a computer can't give the employer a feel for your personality, your communication skills and other characteristics that determine whether or not you'll be a successful fit for the company. As one employer puts it, "The manner in which people present themselves in interviews and relate to me as an interviewer are just as important as the answers they may give to my questions. And you just can't evaluate the human element by looking at a computer printout."

Underneath, they all want the same thing

No two interviews are alike. No two interviewers are alike. But whatever avenues employers take to find out about you, they're all interested in the same thing: Can you solve their problems?

Being a problem-solver today involves more than having the right technical knowledge or ability. You must also exhibit the right attitude and approach toward your work. Here, in no particular order of importance, are three of the most critical qualities employers are seeking today:

- **Cultural fit.** Do you think like others in the organization? Do you have the same work ethic, the same style of management, communication, operation? In other words, will you get along with the gang or will you make trouble? Comments one department director: "There's all this talk today about embracing diversity and disagreement, but in reality, diversity is not embraced, it's reviled." Says another: "You don't get anywhere being a renegade."

- **Focus on the bottom line.** If you want to impress an employer today, you must show that you can make a positive impact on the organization's financial statement. This is true whether you're interviewing with a large corporation or a small nonprofit agency.

- **Enthusiasm for the job.** Surprisingly, many employers rank this as the number-one quality they seek in prospective employees. They say that they would much rather hire a candidate who lacks certain job skills but is very enthusiastic about the job and the company than a candidate who possesses all the right technical experience but has a poor attitude.

The question, of course, is how do you convince interviewers that you offer all of the above? How do you sell yourself to different types of interviewers and in different types of interviews? You'll learn the answers to these and other questions in the coming chapters.

Chapter 6

Sales training 101

If you ever sold a product or service for a living, you're one step ahead when it comes to job interviews. For the job interview is, in essence, a sales call. You're there to sell a product: you. You must convince the customer—the employer—to buy your services.

Some people find this concept offensive. They think it's crass to talk about human beings as commodities to be bought and sold. But the truth is that when employers hire workers, they exchange cash for services, just as you exchange your money for a haircut or a brake job. And the mental process they go through is the same one you use to select a hairdresser or mechanic.

Over the years, researchers and marketers have studied how people make purchase decisions. Through this research, they discovered that there are specific things salespeople can do to increase their odds of success. It doesn't matter whether the salesperson is pushing cold cream, cars or caviar; the same techniques work no matter what the product. They'll work for you, too, as you go to sell your product to employers.

This chapter explores these proven sales techniques and explains why they make you more attractive to employers. You also get a look at the hiring process from the employer's point of view, which tells you a lot about the right things to say and do during your interviews.

Why they buy

Research studies show that people buy a product or service only when:

1. They believe that they have a need or problem.
2. They believe that the product or service is the best solution to that need or problem.

A man might buy a sports car because he sees that particular car as the best way to fill his need for status. A woman might buy a life insurance policy because she believes it's the best way to solve the problem of protecting her family's income. A teenage boy might purchase the hot new style of athletic shoe because he believes he needs the latest gear to win approval from his classmates.

Employers are no different from any other consumer. They won't "buy" you unless they believe that they have a problem and that you're the best solution to that problem. It's your job to lead the employer to this conclusion.

Know your customer

When marketers develop a sales campaign, the first thing they do is research their targeted customer. They gather information about the customer's likes and dislikes. They determine what problems are uppermost in the customer's mind. They find out what sort of solution is most attractive to the customer. Then they devise a sales message that appeals to the attitudes and concerns of the customer.

The smart job-hunter does the same thing. You need to find out everything you can about a prospective employer before your interview. What problems is the employer trying to solve? What skills and experience does the employer think are required to solve those problems? What personality traits and work habits does the company value—that is, what type of a "solution" does the employer prefer to hire?

With this information in hand, you can custom-tailor your sales pitch to the employer. You can be sure that you discuss the skills, experience and qualifications that are of most interest to the buyer.

Imagine that you're interviewing for a job in telemarketing. Through your research, you learn that the company is having trouble matching its competitor in terms of customer service. This tells you that in addition to emphasizing your superb sales record during your interview, you should also stress your customer-relations skills.

Keep in mind that if you interview with several different people at the same company, each person may have a different agenda. To the telemarketing director, an increase in sales might be the top priority, while the quality assurance manager might regard customer service as more important. As an astute salesperson, you must assess each interviewer and adapt your sales pitch accordingly. Ideally, you should find out ahead of time who will be interviewing you and then talk with your networking contacts to learn a little about each of those people.

Getting to know your customer gives you another advantage during your interviews, too. When you display knowledge about the employer, you show the interviewer that you're interested in the job and the company. More importantly, you show that you have an understanding of the company's needs and problems. Employers say that they look for this characteristic in potential job candidates. They also say that arriving at the interview without any background information about the company is one of the biggest and most common mistakes made by job-hunters today.

Focus on their needs, not yours

The mind of the consumer is a selfish one. We don't care about the needs or the problems of the seller. All we want to know is, "What's in it for me?"

Suppose you see a newspaper ad announcing a sale at your favorite department store. The ad proclaims, "We need to reduce our inventory to avoid paying a huge tax bill!" If you decide to check out the sale, it's not because you care about the store's looming tax burden. It's because you determine that there's something in it for you—in this case, lower prices.

Similarly, employers don't care much about your needs or problems. They're only interested in what you can do for them. They may ask about your long-term career aspirations, but they only do so to evaluate your personality and to find out whether your desires might affect them either positively or negatively. They're not in business to help you realize your dreams, after all; they're in business to accomplish their goals.

Too many job-hunters are oblivious to this fact. Instead of focusing on the employer's problems, they focus on their own needs. For example, consider the following scenario: An employer, interviewing candidates for the position of administrative assistant, mentions that the company needs someone who can help other employees learn a new computer program. The uninformed interviewee might respond with something like, "Oh, that's fine. I like that program. Computers are really interesting to me."

What's wrong with such a response? Everything. The interviewer didn't make the statement about needing a computer trainer to find out whether the job candidate would enjoy that aspect of the job. The concern is whether the candidate can solve the problem. So a much more effective answer is, "I can be a big help in that area because I'm very familiar with that particular program."

If you want to capture the interviewer's heart, keep your interview responses "you-based," not "me-based." In other words, focus on the needs of the buyer and not the seller.

Prove your value

As mentioned earlier, you must convince the interviewer that you're the best solution to the company's needs. The key word here is "prove." You can't just say that you're great at something; you must provide hard evidence that backs up your claim. In addition, you must help the interviewer understand how a particular skill or quality enables you to solve the company's problems. Here's how to do that.

1. Talk about your accomplishments

When you present your skills and experience to an interviewer, don't just rattle off a list of past jobs and responsibilities.

Rather, describe in detail what you accomplished in each of those jobs.

Let's say you're interviewing for a job as manager in a bookstore, and the interviewer says, "Tell me about your last job." You answer:

> *"I've been a bookseller at Pepple Books for the past two years."*

The problem with this response is that it only tells the interviewer what you did. It doesn't explain how well you did it or how your efforts affected the company's profits. A more effective approach is to say something like:

> *"For the past two years, I've been a bookseller at Pepple Books. During that time, I've accomplished a number of things that should help me succeed at your store. For example, from what you've told me, the assistant manager will be responsible for inventory management. I helped create an inventory management system for Pepple Books that reduced the time it took us to produce inventory reports by 40 percent."*

When you describe your accomplishments, always do so in terms of the bottom line. Talk about how you cut expenses, increased revenues, strengthened customer relations or reduced the number of hours required to perform a particular task. As much as possible, give specific numbers: You cut expenses by 30 percent, brought in $50,000 worth of new business, increased customer-satisfaction ratings from 3 to 7 on a scale of 10. Always remember that one of the most important things to employers today is whether you demonstrate a clear focus on company profitability.

2. Why did you do it that way?

It's also important to explain why you did what you did the way you did it. This demonstrates to the interviewer that you're able to think through a problem and then uncover a solution. It also proves that your accomplishments were the result of your own intelligence and hard work, rather than some outside factor.

Jeff Bell, who interviewed candidates for supervisory positions at a large international travel-services corporation, recalls his reaction to job applicants who didn't explain the logic behind their on-the-job decisions: "If they couldn't tell me why they handled a certain issue the way they did, I tended to think, 'Gee, you haven't really thought through the management process.' There was a question in my mind about whether they had just gotten lucky or whether they really knew what they were doing."

Bell adds that in his experience, women tended to leave out this information more than men. "With female job candidates, I usually had to ask, 'Why did you come to that decision?' Men were generally more forthcoming. The women that I hired were those who could explain in a little more detail not only what they did, but why they did the things they did."

3. You don't have any accomplishments?

When I help friends put together resumes or prepare for interviews, one of the first questions I ask is, "What are some of your important accomplishments?" Nine times out of 10, their response is, "I really don't have any." But after a little prodding, they invariably come up with all sorts of impressive achievements.

If, while reading the preceding sections, you've been thinking to yourself that you don't have any accomplishments worth mentioning, I can guarantee you that you're wrong. Perhaps you simply haven't given it enough thought, or—more likely—you decided that if you accomplished something, it must not have been a very big deal or that you simply got lucky. Women, especially, are notorious for this kind of self-deprecating thinking.

No matter how you spent the last five years, whether you've been working in the corporate arena, going to school or raising a family, you accomplished many worthwhile things. All you need to do is go looking for them—and refuse to dismiss them as unimportant when you find them. The exercises in Chapter 11 will help you develop your list of accomplishments and understand their value to potential employers.

Sell benefits, not just features

One of the basic tenets of sales theory is that as you describe the features of a product, you must explain how the customer will benefit from those features. If you're selling sweaters, you don't just tell the customer, "This sweater is made of a cotton/polyester blend." Instead, you say, "This sweater is made of a cotton/polyester blend, which means that you can wash it in the washing machine. You won't have to spend money on dry cleaning."

Explaining advantages and benefits in this way helps reinforce the idea that the product is the answer to the customer's needs. It also helps customers visualize themselves using the product and benefiting from it.

You, too, must help your potential buyers understand exactly how they'll benefit from your professional "features"— your skills, experience and other qualifications. For example, imagine that you're interviewing for the position of computer sales representative for XYZ Corporation's Eastern U.S. sales territory. Instead of simply saying, "I have five years experience in computer sales," you must explain how that experience will affect the employer's cash flow:

> "For the past five years, I've been selling computers for ABC Systems. This experience helped me develop very strong sales techniques, to the point that last year I was the top producer in my sales district. I believe that I could use these same skills to help you build your business in the Eastern territory, because both positions involve selling to large industrial clients."

Don't assume that interviewers will understand how you can benefit the company just by looking at your resume. Help them make the connection by explaining exactly what each of your skills, accomplishments or qualifications can mean to them.

Anticipate objections

People who train others in the art of selling have a favorite saying: "The sale begins when the customer says no." The theory behind this motto is that when customers say the product isn't right for them, the sale isn't necessarily dead. It simply means that the salesperson needs to find out what it is about the product that the buyer doesn't like and then discuss features and benefits that address those concerns.

You should use this strategy, known as overcoming objections, in your interviews. Before your interview, think about what concerns the interviewer is likely to have about you. Are you weak at a particular skill on the employer's list of job requirements? Are you older or younger than the typical candidate for a position at this level? Do you lack actual work experience in this particular field or industry? After you identify these potential objections, develop responses that help overcome them.

Let me give you an example that illustrates the concept of overcoming objections. During a promotional tour for the first *Smart Woman* book, I stopped at a cafe for a cup of coffee. At the next table, two business owners were interviewing a young woman for a sales job. One of the owners asked the candidate if she had any sales experience other than spending the past six months as a clerk at a retail store. It was clear from the expression on the owner's face and the tone of his voice that he wasn't happy about such limited experience. But instead of reassuring the owner that she could do the job, the applicant simply said, "No, I really don't. This is my first sales job." She reinforced the owner's objection to her lack of experience.

What would have been a better response? How about:

> "My experience at selling a retail product has come from my current job. But during my other jobs, I've often had to sell ideas or programs. For example, I put together a proposal that convinced the company president that we could cut back on mailing expenses if we changed our shipping procedures. This was quite a big sales job, because the new procedures were a major departure from the current system. The techniques and strategies that I used to sell the proposal are the same ones that I use to sell products on my job today. So although I only have six months of retail-sales experience, I do have a lot of sales knowledge. And as my current boss will tell you, I'm also a quick learner."

In addition to preparing responses to possible objections before the interview, you must listen carefully during the interview to uncover interviewer concerns. Sometimes, objections aren't expressly stated, but hidden in the conversation. These are called hidden objections.

Several years ago, I interviewed for the position of marketing director for a small company. One of the interviewers kept stressing that the organization needed someone who was financially astute. He never came right out and said, "I don't think you have enough financial experience," but his repetition of the organization's accounting and budgeting needs was a clear signal that he questioned my abilities.

To address his concerns, I said something to the effect of:

> *"You know, because my resume focuses heavily on my marketing and PR background, you might have questions about my finance-management skills. I can tell you that in my last job, I was responsible for writing the annual budget, overseeing department purchases and negotiating prices with vendors. During my two years in that job, I was able to make the department a profit center for the first time in company history."*

This must have calmed his fears, because later, the company president said that I had impressed the financial guru. It's doubtful that would have happened if I hadn't picked up on his objections during the interview.

In Chapter 11, you'll create a list of the possible concerns your potential customer might have about you and develop responses that will help you overcome those objections.

Ask for the sale

Another major lesson of Sales Training 101 is that you must always ask for the sale. The same is true for interviews: If you want the job, say so at the end of the interview.

A friend of mine who works in sales recently took this tactic to an extreme. The executive recruiter with whom he had registered advised him to conclude every interview by pushing for a job offer. "Be cocky," the recruiter said. "Be a little arrogant."

My friend tried this technique not once, but three times. At the close of the interview, he said:

"I really like what I hear about this job, and I think you like me as well. So I'd like to leave here today with a commitment from you. What do you say?"

All three interviewers were initially taken aback by my friend's boldness. But then, all three broke into huge grins and said something like, "Well, we can't give you an offer today. But we like the fact that you tried to 'close' us. It shows that you would be a strong closer, which is what our sales force needs."

It's very important that you understand that I'm not recommending this approach unless you are interviewing for a sales position in which you would be expected to use high-pressure closing on the job. Even if you are applying for a sales position, back off immediately if the interviewer says that closing the deal that day is not possible. This is not the place for heavy-handed closing tactics. The last thing you want to do is back the interviewer into an uncomfortable corner.

In most cases, it's best to find a middle ground between being too pushy and appearing so blasé that you give the interviewer the impression you're not interested. Here's an example:

"I'm really enthusiastic about this job. Can you please tell me where you are in the interviewing process and when I can expect a response from you?"

Such closing statements are good because they not only display your interest in the position but also demonstrate that you're proactively managing your job search. You let interviewers know that the ball is in their court, but you also let them know that this is one of several possibilities you're considering.

Listen

During job interviews, it's easy to be so focused on what you want to tell the interviewer that you forget to listen. Listening to what the interviewer is saying is just as important as describing your qualifications and skills. In order to determine what the employer's needs are and how you can meet those needs, you must pay attention not only to the spoken word, but also to the interviewer's body language and unspoken concerns.

Women probably have an edge in this regard; our culture casts women in the role of listener more often than not, so we have a lot of practice at it. However, it is possible to listen too much and talk too little. If the interviewer does all of the talking and you do all of the listening, it can be viewed as a sign of weakness. Try to strike an even balance between listening and talking.

Clarify vague questions

When you're asked a vague or very general question, be sure to pinpoint the interviewer's concern before you answer. A case in point is the question, "How do you handle stress?" The interviewer might be concerned that you won't be able to handle the heavy workload. Then again, that might not be the concern at all. It could be that the interviewer is worried about your ability to deal with messy internal politics, unsatisfied customers, cramped working conditions or any number of other stress-provoking situations.

You could simply answer, "Stress doesn't bother me." But on its own, that's a pretty weak statement, and you can't describe accomplishments or past experiences that prove to the interviewer you can deal with the problem until you're sure exactly what the problem is. It's vital that you clarify what information the interviewer is really seeking. You might say something like:

> "Well, stress can come from a variety of different directions, and I use different skills to handle different types of stress. Could you explain what stressful situations I would be expected to handle? Then I can better explain to you how I would cope."

Don't be afraid to ask for this clarification; it will help both you and the interviewer find out exactly what you need to know about each other.

Be confident in your product

One of the most important things you can do to improve your chances of making a sale is to speak and act in a confident manner. You're right—that's easier said than done. But if you don't believe in your product, why should the employer?

In Chapter 9, you'll learn some tricks you can use to make yourself appear more confident even when you're quaking inside. In the meantime, make a vow right now to become your own best cheerleader. Instead of thinking about all the things you don't have to offer an employer, concentrate on all those things you do well. Think about what you would say to a friend or family member who was about to interview for a job. You'd find all sorts of encouraging words and compliments! Start saying all those nice things to yourself.

It takes practice

There's one important element of effective selling we haven't discussed yet: establishing rapport—better known as "chemistry"—with the customer. There's an art to creating chemistry, and you'll learn how to do it in the next chapter.

But before wrapping up this chapter, I want to emphasize two things. First, remember that the sales techniques you just read about aren't radical new ideas. They're time-honored, proven concepts. Oddly enough, most job-hunters don't incorporate them into their interview presentations. Why not? Because most people are uncomfortable selling themselves. Which brings us to the second point: You probably won't feel totally at ease saying and doing the things you read about in this chapter, either—at first.

For that reason, it's vital that you practice, practice, practice. Just as salespeople rehearse their sales pitches until they've got them down cold, you must rehearse your sales statements until you can say them without discomfort. The more you practice, the easier it will be to sell yourself in job interviews.

Chapter 7

Creating chemistry

One of the most frustrating aspects of job interviews is the degree to which personal chemistry affects your success or failure. You can be the most qualified person for the job, present the most impressive references, say and do all the right things during your interview, but if the chemistry between you and the interviewer is bad, there's no way you'll get the job.

Even though hiring managers and HR specialists say they try to maintain their objectivity during the selection process, most admit that chemistry plays a huge role in the way they respond to job candidates. Some say that chemistry accounts for as much as 50 percent of their hiring decisions!

The last chapter discussed the fact that the job interview is essentially a sales call and that the techniques used by professional salespeople to increase their success rate can help you sell yourself more effectively to interviewers. The same parallel exists with interview chemistry.

Smart salespeople understand that their chances of making a sale are much greater when the chemistry between seller and buyer is good. They also know that although some aspects of personal chemistry are beyond their control, they can use certain tactics to "create chemistry" with potential customers. These strategies will help you build rapport with interviewers, too.

The chemical equation

It's important to distinguish between the kind of chemistry that makes for a successful job interview and the kind you read about in romance novels. When we talk about interview chemistry, we're not talking about that weak-in-the-knees, heart-stopping zing we associate with love at first sight.

Interview chemistry can perhaps best be described as a mutual feeling of professional respect. It happens when you and the interviewer realize that you share the same professional attitudes, ideas and goals. You both say to yourself, "Aha! This person thinks like I do. We could work together well."

But interview chemistry involves more than a shared professional ideology. When two people click, they usually share some personal characteristics, too. They may speak at the same rate, have the same sense of humor—even use the same body language.

In personal relationships, the old maxim is, "opposites attract." The reverse is true for interviewer/interviewee relationships. As discussed in Chapter 1, researchers say that interviewers tend to hire people like themselves. So the more your behavior and thought process matches that of the interviewer, the better the interview chemistry.

Why chemistry is so important

During the typical hiring process, interviewers are called upon to make fairly quick judgments about the candidates they meet. In many cases, interviewers have only 30 minutes to approve or reject a potential employee. Obviously, that's not enough time to gather a great deal of hard information. So interviewers usually rely heavily on gut instinct in deciding whether to pursue a job candidate further. Chemistry plays a big part in the formation of that instinct.

The extent to which chemistry affects the hiring decision depends in part upon the skill of the interviewer, say career consultants and HR experts. The better the interviewer, the more objective the hiring decision is likely to be. When interviewers are unskilled or inexperienced, chemistry plays a much bigger role in the employment process.

At some level, though, chemistry affects your interview even if the interviewer is a seasoned veteran. Interviewers are human, after all, and human nature says we respond better to people when we feel a certain "connection" with them.

Good news for women

Most experts think that women are much better at creating chemistry than men. Why? In part, because we're culturally conditioned to be better at reading people and adapting our behavior accordingly. In addition, women tend to be more open and honest, which also fosters good communication. (Even when we're not being totally up-front, generations of social stereotyping lead most interviewers to perceive women as being more honest than men.)

Adapt your communication style

Aside from being born a woman, what can you do to create chemistry with interviewers? The first strategy is to alter your communication style to match that of the interviewer.

As explained earlier in this chapter, the amount of chemistry between an interviewer and interviewee depends in part upon how many professional and personal traits you share. For that reason, interviewers are likely to respond better if you communicate using the same pace, tone and body language as they do.

"You have to have your antenna up and take signals from the interviewer," says Marcia Glatman, president of HRD Consultants Inc., a New Jersey executive-search firm. "Say, for example, that the interviewer is a very fast talker, uses a shotgun approach to asking questions and exudes a lot of energy. If you sit there slumped in your chair and talk very slowly, that won't go over very well. You have to shift your communication style to that of the interviewer."

At the beginning of the interview, take note of the interviewer's communication style and then adapt your own delivery to match that style. If the interviewer fires off comments at a breakneck pace and you normally talk in slow, measured tones, pick up your delivery a bit. If the interviewer is very soft-spoken, keep your voice level down as well. If the interviewer is very animated and moves around a lot while speaking, use some hand gestures of your own.

You'll be more likely to connect with interviewers if you adopt their "personality" a bit, too. If they're very casual and relaxed, for instance, and you act very stiff and reserved, they'll feel uncomfortable with you, because your personality appears very different from theirs. If, on the other hand, you adopt the same informal, relaxed style, you help them come to the conclusion that "this person is just like me."

You can pick up cues about personality from the interviewer's body language, verbal statements, dress and—presuming your discussion takes place in the interviewer's office—from the office environment. If there's not a bit of clutter anywhere on the interviewer's desk, chances are you're dealing with a very controlled, detail-oriented person. If the interviewer begins the meeting by saying, "Let's get right down to brass tacks; tell me about your qualifications," you know that this is not a person who values the pleasantries of small talk.

Speak their language

In addition to mirroring the interviewer's personality and communication styles, it's also important to tailor your presentation to suit the interviewer's level of knowledge about your particular field.

In most cases, HR interviewers are less familiar with the technical side of the position than the direct hiring manager. To improve your communication with them, avoid using buzzwords or acronyms that may be meaningless to someone without your technical training. Express your qualifications and experience in terms a layperson can understand, without being condescending.

When you interview with the hiring manager, however, do use the technical terminology of your field. Just be sure that you're using current buzzwords—they tend to become popular and then *passè* in a very short time. If you've been out of the work force for a while, read some trade magazines before your interview to acquaint yourself with the latest lingo.

No matter what the technical background of the interviewer, however, you can endear yourself by using one particular word: the interviewer's name. Human beings are an egotistical bunch, and we love to hear our own names. Don't overdo it, starting off every sentence with the interviewer's name, but do throw it in once or twice during the interview and definitely in your closing statement. If you are roughly the same age as your interviewers, it's probably okay to address them by their first names if they call you by your first name. Take your cue from how interviewers introduce themselves to you. When the interviewer is much older than you, it's best not to assume that a first-name basis is appropriate; use the titles "Mr. Jones" or "Ms. Jones" unless the interviewer indicates otherwise. If the interviewer has a professional title, such as Dr. or Reverend, be sure to use it.

Make a good first impression

During the first few minutes of the interview, the interviewer makes certain judgments about your character and workstyle. These judgments, based on your dress, demeanor and body language, have a great effect on how much chemistry you'll be able to establish during the remainder of your interview.

If interviewers perceive you as a polished, capable professional, they tend to relax a bit and relate to you more warmly. If, however, the first impression you make is a negative one, they'll probably respond negatively to everything else you have to say. You certainly won't be able to establish any chemistry with them; even if the two of you do have something in common, the interviewer won't acknowledge it. Who wants to admit that they share personality traits with someone they judge as less than professional?

Chapter 8 discusses in detail the art of creating a good first impression. But to sum up briefly, you must:

- **Observe interview etiquette.** Be on time; sit when and where the interviewer indicates; and don't smoke, chew gum or eat during your meeting.

- **Greet everyone in a warm, enthusiastic manner.**
  Smile and offer a firm, friendly handshake.
- **Adopt confident body language.** Maintain good
  eye contact, control your nervous mannerisms and
  watch your posture. Don't slouch.
- **Dress for business.** Be sure that everything about
  your appearance, from your hair to your clothing to
  your fingernails, tells the interviewer, "Here's a com-
  petent professional."

Don't lose yourself in the process

Does all of this mean that you should attempt to act like a
clone of your interviewers—to hide your own personality and
take on theirs? Definitely not. It's a rare individual who can
perform this chameleon-like transformation without appearing phony. Interviewers know when they're being snowed.

Creating chemistry doesn't mean trying to fool the interviewer into thinking you're something that you're not. It
means setting a positive climate for your interaction by making a good first impression and respecting the interviewer's
personal and professional style. It also means paying attention
to signals that tell you what sort of communication is most
comfortable for the interviewer, and then relating in that manner. Your goal is to help make the other person more comfortable and to find areas of common ground so that your conversation can be a relaxed, open and productive exchange of
information.

The dangers of too much chemistry

Sometimes, the chemistry between you and the interviewer will be so terrific that you'll feel like you're talking with
an old friend. That's good—but it's also dangerous.

"People can get so relaxed that they forget they're in an
interview," explains Marcia Glatman. "They talk too much,
reveal things they shouldn't." Glatman adds that skilled interviewers try to make interviewees feel very relaxed. "They're
good at asking you the hard questions while making you feel

very comfortable. You must always bear in mind that you're in a job interview. You're talking with an interviewer, not a friend, so pay attention to what you say."

Too much chemistry can also be a problem with unskilled interviewers. If the personal chemistry is very good between you and the interviewer, the conversation may drift from business to personal issues, especially when interviewer and interviewee are uncomfortable with the interview process. It's easier to talk about children or hobbies than it is to ask and answer those hard-core interview questions.

Such an interview may seem more pleasant to you, but it probably hurts your chances of being hired. If you spend all your time talking about nonbusiness matters, the interviewer leaves the meeting without any real sense of your professional qualifications. The interviewer might be sold on you as a person, but not as a solution to the company's business problems.

This scenario often crops up when women interview with men who aren't really comfortable dealing with women on a professional level. Instead of discussing business issues, such interviewers bring up things they think the woman can relate to—for example, they launch into a discussion about local schools or baby sitters.

If this happens to you—regardless of whether the interviewer is a man or woman—it's important to get the conversation back on a business track. As soon as possible, say something like, "Getting back to one particular area of the company you mentioned..." Do this politely and with a smile, but do it. Otherwise, the interviewer will learn your feelings about schools and baby-sitting as opposed to learning about your accomplishments and abilities.

You already have good chemistry skills

If you're unsure about your ability to create chemistry, or if you worry that it's just too much to think about chemistry and your interview answers, remember that you already possess rapport-building skills. In fact, you create chemistry with friends and family every day. For example, you probably use a totally different rate and style of speech with an elderly grandparent than you use with a teenage relative. You automatically adjust your communication style in reaction to the other person.

Creating chemistry in interviews is simply a matter of doing the same thing, only faster. In personal relationships, you have years to determine the best ways of communicating with people. In interviews, you must assess the other person in a matter of minutes. The secret is to turn up your interpersonal radar a few notches so that you can pick up all those subtle signals the interviewer sends.

Now that you understand the basics of creating chemistry, let's return for a closer look at a subject we touched on briefly in this chapter: making a good first impression.

Chapter 8

Making a good first impression

Researchers say that interviewers make a judgment about job applicants during the first five or 10 minutes of the interview. They also say that once that judgment is made, it seldom changes. Clearly, first impressions count—a lot.

What can you do to create a good first impression? This chapter outlines the basic do's and don'ts.

1. Dress for business

Your appearance is perhaps the most critical element of building a positive first impression. Employers assume that what they see is what they'll get if they hire you, so make sure that what they see is a consummate professional. Walk in to the interview in stirrup pants and a sweater, shorts and a T-shirt or, even worse, a low-cut blouse and miniskirt, and you immediately make a negative statement. Without saying a word, you're less attractive to the employer than candidates who arrive in a proper business suit. Understand that dressing professionally is one of the rules of the business game. Don't expect to win the game if you break that rule.

Granted, it's more difficult for a woman to decide what constitutes proper business attire than it is for a man. A man simply pulls on the time-honored uniform: a black or dark-blue suit and conservative tie. A while back, in an attempt to create their own version of the uniform, many women took to wearing navy suits and little bow ties that were supposed to mimic the man's power tie. Unfortunately for those who filled up their closets with navy suits and bow ties, that answer to the business-wear dilemma is now considered outdated.

So what are you supposed to wear? Aim for a look that's stylish but conservative. Wear a fashionable business suit in a low-key color, a minimum of jewelry, simple accessories and low-heeled pumps. No low-cut or sheer blouses. No spike heels or sandals. No little-girlish jumpers and no nightclub-hopping mini-skirts or stretch pants. Always dress as if you're interviewing for the CEO's job, no matter what position you're seeking.

If you work in one of the "creative" fields—advertising, art and the like—don't make the mistake of wearing your most avant-garde garb in an effort to show your creative genius. Let your portfolio do the talking in that regard. Your appearance should tell the interviewer that you also have a head for business.

Keep in mind that for women, business fashions change often. If you're not certain what's considered "stylish and conservative" at the moment, pick up a copy of *Working Woman* or a similar publication and scan the fashion pages. If you don't own anything that's suitable and can't afford a new outfit, borrow from your professional friends. Shopping resale boutiques is another great option; often, you can pick up barely worn designer suits for next-to-nothing.

2. Pay attention to details

Interviewers notice the little things. Sloppy manicures, missing buttons, scuffed shoes, stained lapels or snagged stockings are interpreted as signs that the candidate isn't detail-oriented. So make sure that your entire outfit is impeccably clean and neat.

For women, makeup is often a downfall. Keep yours subtle: no clown cheeks, iridescent eye shadow, inch-long lashes or glossy purple lipstick. Opt for short nails with clear or pale polish; loud colors, especially bright reds and pinks, denote a yen for parties rather than business.

Again, if you're not sure what's acceptable, consult a business magazine (the *Cosmopolitan* "night-on-the-town" look is not what you're after). You might also want to ask a friend whose opinion you respect to critique your look.

3. Don't wear cologne or perfume

Nearly all of the interviewers I surveyed mentioned cologne-overkill as one of the biggest gaffes made by both male and female job candidates. In fact, many interviewers rated this as their number-one gripe!

It's nearly impossible to tell how strong an odor your own perfume or cologne is emitting. What seems like a pleasant whiff of scent to you may overpower someone else. So why risk it? Don't wear any scent at all. No, one little dab or spritz is not okay. Put that bottle down.

Another smell-related note: If you're a smoker, avoid smoking in the hours before your interview. At the very least, don't smoke in your interview outfit. Employers generally regard smoking as an undesirable habit, and cigarette odors cling to clothes for hours. Your nose might not pick it up, but the non-smoker's surely will.

4. Watch your body language

As they're forming an impression of you, interviewers also observe your body language for clues about your personality, credibility and confidence. Here's a rundown of the most common body-language signals and what they mean to interviewers.

Look them in the eye

In American culture, the ability to look someone in the eye is interpreted as a sign of honesty. For that reason, interviewers react negatively to job candidates who can't maintain a reasonable amount of eye contact. This doesn't mean, however, that you should get into a staring contest with the interviewer. Constant, unblinking eye contact quickly becomes invasive and uncomfortable. Try to maintain the same amount of eye contact as you do when talking with a good friend.

Greet the interviewer with a firm handshake

Again, because of cultural stereotypes, someone who has a firm handshake is regarded as confident and authoritative; someone with a "limp-fish" handshake is regarded as—well, a limp fish.

Even though a handshake may seem like a small element on which to base a decision about someone's character, interviewers really do read a lot into it. Moreover, they usually remember your handshake long after they've forgotten what you said during the interview. "If the candidate had a weak handshake, you can bet it will come up when a group of people get together to discuss a candidate after an interview," said one hiring manager.

As with eye contact, though, it's important not to go overboard in your efforts to avoid the limp-fish shake. It's not acceptable to crush the other person's fingers. A nice, firm clasp will do. If you're not accustomed to shaking hands in your daily life, practice with a few friends and get their feedback.

Don't fidget

After the publication of the first *Smart Woman* book, I was asked to appear on a television talk show. It was my first on-camera appearance, and needless to say, I was more than a little nervous. As the interview progressed, however, I thought I was doing a pretty good job of controlling my nerves. My answers (at least to me) seemed calm and confident.

Later, when I watched a tape of the show, I was appalled to see that the entire time I was speaking, I was swinging my foot wildly back and forth (I had been sitting with my legs crossed at the knees). I kicked that foot up and down, back and forth, in, out, in, out—it's a wonder I didn't fling a shoe across the stage. I have since learned that my nervous energy tends to come out through my feet, so I take special care to keep them firmly planted during tense situations.

Be careful that your body language doesn't betray your nervousness in the same way during your interviews. In addition to leg-swinging, avoid these other mannerisms that interviewers perceive as signs of nervousness:

- Touching your hair repeatedly.
- Placing your hand near your mouth or around your face as you talk (also seen as a sign of dishonesty).
- Clearing your throat continually.
- Tapping your fingers or (worse) cracking your knuckles.
- Playing with your jewelry or frequently adjusting your glasses.

If you feel your body getting out of control, try focusing on your breathing: Taking steady, deep breaths will help you relax. It's also good to take a short walk before your interview to burn off some of that nervous energy.

Sit forward in your chair

Interviewers take note of how candidates sit during the interview. Candidates who slump in their chairs or appear too relaxed are perceived as either unconfident or unmotivated or both. Candidates who sit up straight and lean a little bit forward in their chairs are perceived as attentive and interested in the job.

5. Respect the rules of interview etiquette

Just as there are rules of etiquette for social interactions, there are rules of etiquette for the interaction we call the job interview. Although these rules may seem unimportant to you, they are very important to interviewers. Employers assume that if you don't know anything about interview etiquette, you may not understand the rules of everyday-business etiquette, either.

Be on time

One of the basic laws of interview etiquette—and one that's broken with surprisingly regularity—is to arrive on time. Allow plenty of extra time to get to your interview; you never know when a traffic jam or other transportation catastrophe is going to occur. (Arriving early also gives you a chance to calm your nerves a bit before the interview begins.) If you run late because of some unavoidable problem, call ahead to let the interviewer know. Apologize profusely and ask whether the interviewer would prefer to reschedule.

Remember that you're the guest

Interview etiquette also says that you are the guest and the interviewer is the host. So don't sit down until the interviewer invites you to do so. Don't plop your briefcase down on the interviewer's desk, and don't start fingering any office knickknacks, even if it's one of those inviting little stress-relief gizmos. And if you think the wallpaper is tacky or the view of the parking lot is less than attractive, for heaven's sake don't say so.

A special word of caution to women: If you spy family pictures on the interviewer's desk, resist the urge to comment, even though you might naturally do so if you were visiting that person's home. Raising the issue of families and children is something you want to avoid in an interview. If the interviewer is a strong family-values person, a compliment about the beautiful children may succeed in creating a bond of sorts by showing that you think families are important, too. But it also reinforces any perceptions the interviewer might have about women's preference for family life over professional life. Remember, your goal here is to show that you think work is important.

Don't smoke, chew gum or eat

Never light up a cigarette during an interview, even if the interviewer indulges in chain-smoking. Employers are very concerned about employee health today, and most people— even smokers—consider smoking to be a sign of poor health habits.

Don't have anything else in your mouth during the interview, either. That includes mints, gum and the rest of your soft drink from lunch. (I actually interviewed one job candidate who slurped his soda through a straw during our entire discussion.) If the interviewer offers you a cup of coffee or other beverage, of course, feel free to accept if you're so inclined. My own personal practice, however, is to decline such offers; I've learned that doing so greatly reduces the chance that I'll spill my drink all over the interviewer's desk.

Don't dismiss anyone

Be friendly, polite and respectful toward everyone you meet, from the receptionist at the front door to the interviewer's secretary. There's a good chance that all of these people will be asked to offer an opinion about you. So treat every encounter as a "silent interview."

6. Be enthusiastic

As mentioned in earlier chapters, nearly all of the hiring managers who shared their insights with me said that one of the first things they notice is the amount of enthusiasm a job candidate displays. Many said it was the most important element in whether they left the interview with a positive impression of the candidate.

Forget any notions you may have that playing hard-to-get will somehow make the interviewer want you more. Acting indifferent may be a wonderful tactic for attracting romantic partners—in games of love, it seems, we always want what we think we can't have. But appear laid-back, uninterested or bored with an interviewer, and you're dead in the water.

Now for the hard part

As you can see, creating a good first impression is mostly a matter of common sense. Pay attention to your appearance, your mannerisms and your manners, and you'll go a long way toward convincing interviewers that you're the kind of professional they want to hire.

After you create that first impression, of course, you must reinforce it with a strong sales presentation. You must show the interviewer that you not only can look and act the part, but that you also have the skills and experience to solve the company's problems.

If you're like most job-seekers, this is the hardest part of interviewing. You may find it difficult to speak about your abilities—perhaps it seems embarrassing to you, or perhaps you simply aren't sure that you actually have any abilities. Or you may not understand how to describe your qualifications in terms that make an impact with interviewers. Never fear. In the next chapter, you'll find advice on how to develop a confident, powerful interviewing style.

Chapter 9

Selling yourself with confidence

At the beginning of the movie *The Sound of Music*, there's a scene in which the Julie Andrews character, Maria, makes her way toward the home of the intimidating Captain Von Trapp, where she is to try her hand at being a governess. Having just been booted from her job as a nun because her superiors didn't think she was cut out for abbey life, Maria's a bit of a wreck. Full of self-doubt and anxiety, she's not sure that she has what it takes to be a governess either.

Then, as characters in musicals are prone to do, Maria bursts into song, launching into the tune "I Have Confidence" in an attempt to boost her self-esteem. Actually, she doesn't really burst into this particular song; she begins it in a weak, uncertain tone. But after a few bars, she's in clear and powerful voice, announcing to the world that she's confident she can do the job. She vows to impress her new employer, to show the world that she's worthy. By the time she wraps up the song and knocks on the Captain's door, she's transformed from cowering ex-nun to confident, I-can-do-anything woman.

That movie image—of Maria standing on the doorstep, confident, enthusiastic and smiling—is the perfect description of the attitude you should project when you knock on the door of your prospective employer. From the moment you meet your interviewers until the time you say good-bye, everything about you must say, "I'm confident in my ability to do this job well." If you don't speak and act as if you have confidence in your abilities, don't expect the interviewer to have any confidence in you, either.

The language of self-confidence

Many women, especially those who haven't spent much time in the work force, have great difficulty in this department. Some men also suffer from a lack of self-esteem, of course, but women are generally more prone to the problem. And why not? We've grown up in a culture that in many different ways tells us that we're not "as good" as men. Self-confidence is especially a problem for displaced homemakers, who often come to the job search with the frame of mind, "I'm just a housewife."

Exploring the roots of low self-esteem is not the important issue here, however. What matters is that you learn to communicate with interviewers in a calm, confident manner. And here's a little secret: Even if you don't feel confident, you can appear confident. Simply by mimicking the language patterns of confident people and avoiding those patterns used by less-than-confident individuals, you can create an image of confidence.

According to researchers, people who have low self-esteem tend to use some of the following language patterns, which reveal a lack of confidence.

1. Hedges and qualifiers

Whereas confident people say, "I think that's wrong" or "We should do it this way," people who have little self-confidence say, "I sort of think we might be better off with this approach" or "I think this would be a good idea, but of course I could be wrong." They state an opinion, but in a weak way that implies, "Excuse me for saying so; I'm not really sure that I know what I'm talking about."

2. Turning statements into questions

People who are short on confidence also tend to phrase what should be statements as questions. The confident person says, "The going rate for a position such as this is $30,000 to $45,000, so I would expect something in that range." The less-assured person turns that statement into a question: "...so I would expect something in that range?" Again, the message is, "I'm not really sure about this, can you reassure me that I'm right?"

3. Expressions of uncertainty

Ask powerful, confident people about their goals, and they'll respond with a statement such as, "I plan to..." or "I will be..." Ask people with low self-esteem the same question, and they'll answer with a statement such as, "Well, I hope to" or "I'm not sure I can do it, but I would like to..." Use the first type of speech, and you demonstrate that you not only are committed to a course of action but are confident you can make it happen. You give just the opposite impression when you pepper your statements with uncertain phrases such as "hope to" and "would like to."

4. Talking too much or too little

Less-than-confident people also tend to either rattle on endlessly, as if afraid of silence, or to clam up so tightly that they barely carry 10 percent of the conversation. Try to maintain a 50-50 split between talking and listening. And don't be so afraid of silence that you rush to answer an interviewer's question without thinking; pause a moment or two to collect your thoughts and then answer. Most interviewers perceive this as a positive sign because it shows that the candidate is really thinking about the question. You can even say, "That's an interesting question. Let me think about that for a moment."

Sociolinguistics experts note that all of these expressions of self-doubt are typical of women's speech patterns. As a little girl, you probably picked up these traits unconsciously because you naturally modeled your own language after other women. So even if you consider yourself a reasonably confident individual, pay attention to your communication style; you may have unwittingly adopted some speech patterns that make you appear less confident than you are. It may be a difficult habit to break, but it's imperative that you banish these strength-sappers from your language if you want to appear confident, powerful and self-assured.

Assume that you have the job

Another way to create a confident interview persona is to ask and answer questions in a way that presumes you already have the job offer. When you ask the interviewer a question about job responsibilities, for example, say, "What will be my major responsibility on this job?" instead of "What will be the major responsibility of the person who gets this job?"

This is a subtle but effective technique. It tells the interviewer that you're confident enough in your abilities to believe that you'll be the best candidate. It also helps interviewers begin to envision you in the job, which, as we discussed in Chapter 6, moves them one step closer to buying your "product."

The power of confident thinking

The more confident you really are, of course, the more automatically you'll display all of the confident speech and behavior patterns we've just discussed. And there's an easy way to put yourself in a confident frame of mind: Think confident thoughts.

Too simplistic for you? Maybe, but it works. Psychologists tell us that thoughts precede emotions. You think something negative about yourself, and pretty soon you start feeling bad about yourself. Fill your brain with positive thoughts about your capabilities, on the other hand, and you start to feel good about yourself. Feeling good about yourself translates into self-confidence.

So, like Maria on her way to the Von Trapp household, tell yourself over and over that you are a capable, intelligent person who has a lot to offer an employer. Feelings of confidence will follow confident thoughts. (I don't recommend, however, that you sing and dance your way up to the employer's front door. In the movies, it's charming; in real life, you're likely to frighten people.)

Don't go overboard

As you develop a more confident communication style, it's important to know when enough is enough. Too much bravado is just as bad as too little. Being confident does not mean being arrogant, pushy, disrespectful or demanding.

It's also a mistake to state your opinions so strongly that you appear inflexible or stubborn. Don't come across as being so steeped in a certain belief that you would never waver from that position. Employers today want people who can adapt to change and who know how to compromise and negotiate with others to achieve common goals.

Some women, aware of the gender discrimination they face and determined not to be taken lightly, go into interviews with guns blazing. They attempt to wow the interviewer with bold, strong language and assertive claims. Unfortunately, this usually backfires. Our society still holds very firm ideas about what language and attitudes are proper for a woman, and if you break those conventions, you'll be perceived as overly aggressive. Unfair, but true.

"The worst thing a woman can do is go into an interview with an attitude," says Nancy Wright-Nelson, president of a Chicago-area executive search firm. "A lot of women think, 'My mother and my older sisters have been put down all their lives, and nobody's going to do that to me. I'm going to let these people know what I'm all about.' The trouble is, it's still a world in which women who take a brazen, very aggressive attitude put people off."

Finding the fine line

So how do you find that fine line between displaying too much confidence and too little? Between being assertive and being aggressive? It's not easy. You must appear confident in your thoughts and actions, but not so much so that you're perceived as a dictator or a stubborn mule instead of a team player.

To complicate the issue further, judgements about what's assertive behavior and what's overly aggressive behavior vary from company to company and from interviewer to interviewer.

95

The same assertive attitude and language that seem perfectly acceptable to a young executive female may be offensive to an older, conservative male. If your interviewer happens to be the latter, it's probably wise to tone down your presentation. That advice may be galling to you, but look at it this way: By playing by the interviewer's rules, you're more likely to get what you want.

Don't assume, however, that only older male interviewers have trouble with assertive women. Remember that women and men hear the very same messages about how women are supposed to act in this world, so a female interviewer may also find assertive behavior unacceptable. You must assess each interviewer, without making any prejudgments or relying on cultural stereotypes, and then decide what level of assertiveness is appropriate. You'll probably have to experiment to find just the right balance of confidence and humility.

As you can see, this is a very fuzzy issue. To help clear things up a bit, here are the responses given by a variety of experts when asked to describe the difference between assertiveness and aggressiveness:

Mary Jo Zaksas, president of Zaksas Associates, a retained search firm:

> *"I think both men and women respect individuals who are strong and confident but who also have a friendly, team-style approach. If the two are together, it works. But if you look like you're just in this for yourself and you're strictly push, push, push, that's going to come across poorly."*

Jane Hassinger, University of Michigan professor of psychology and women's studies:

> *"Assertiveness always keeps the other person in focus, so that your assertion of yourself doesn't cancel out the other person. Aggressiveness cares only about itself and doesn't take into account what the other person may be needing or feeling."*

Mike Matta, director of new business development, R.E. Lowe, a retained and contingency search firm:

> *"The difference between aggressive and assertive is attitude. If you're confident but you have a smile on your face, you're assertive. If you're expressionless, you may appear aggressive."*

Marianne Ruggiero, vice-president of corporate human resources, J. Crew Group, Inc.:

> *"You have to show that when the situation requires, you have the skills and ammunition to get the job done. But you also have to show that you can be adaptable and flexible. So be assertive and be yourself during the interview, but also demonstrate that you know when to be quiet and listen."*

Susan Rettig-Drufke, president, Rettig-Drufke and Associates, a management consultant firm specializing in human resources issues:

> *"The secret is to develop true inner confidence. If you hang on to who you really are and what you can do, you will eventually find the right niche. Your confidence will come through in the right way no matter what words you use."*

I'll also add my own thoughts on the confidence game. To me, the definition in Webster's dictionary hits the nail on the head: "Confidence stresses faith in oneself and one's powers without any suggestion of conceit or arrogance."

The key to acquiring that kind of confidence is to stop comparing yourself with others, either positively or negatively. Think of yourself as an equal of the interviewer and of other candidates for the job—not as being better than this person or not as good as that one. In a competitive society such as ours, that mental approach won't come easy. But if you can master it, confidence will come from within. And when that happens, you won't be so inclined to use expressions of self-doubt to excuse your imagined shortcomings, nor will you feel it necessary to use overly aggressive tactics to prove your worth.

Chapter 10

Interview research: Part 1

The first half of this book focused primarily on the psychological aspects of the interviewing process. That foundation is important because it helps you understand why certain interview techniques work and others get you a quick escort out the door. But now, it's time to get down to the nitty-gritty and begin preparing your actual interview presentation.

This chapter guides you through the first phase of the preparation process, which is to research the company, the job and your market value. As you conduct this research, be sure to write down the information you uncover. You'll need to refer to your research notes when you complete the second part of your interview homework, described in Chapter 11.

Step 1: Research the company

As you learned in Chapter 6, one of the keys to making a sale is getting to know the customer. You must learn about the company's problems, needs and interests so that you can focus your sales presentation on the issues most important to the employer. The more you address those issues in your interview, the greater your chances of getting the job.

Knowing about the employer not only helps you emphasize those skills most relevant to the position, it scores automatic points with the interviewer. Employers are always impressed by candidates who take the time to learn about the company, its products and the industry in general—and they're completely turned off by candidates who don't.

Before your interview, you should know the answers to the following questions (if not more):

- What are the company's major products and services?
- Who are the company's customers?
- How do competitors and customers view the company? (Do they think the company's service is excellent or poor, that products are reasonably priced or a little too expensive?)
- What is the company's standing in the marketplace? Is it a profitable business, or is it teetering on the brink of bankruptcy?
- Who are the company's major competitors?
- What are some of the company's recent success stories?
- What problems is the company trying to solve?
- What is the corporate culture like?
- Is the company privately or publicly owned? Is it an independent organization or part of a larger conglomerate?
- How big is the company? Has it grown or declined over the past five years? (Are they hiring or laying off people?)
- Is the employee turnover rate high, average or low? What factors contribute to that turnover rate? (For example, do people leave the company because of low wages?)
- What is the typical interviewing and hiring process at the company?

To find this information, you have several possible resources, and you should explore them all.

1. Call the company

First, call the company directly. Say that you're interested in learning more about the company and its products, and you'd like to see any annual reports, brochures or other materials that are available. Start with the receptionist or main telephone operator; if those individuals can't help you, they should know who can. If the company has a public relations department, try that avenue, too. Sometimes, you can get your hands on employee magazines or newsletters, which can provide a wealth of behind-the-scenes information.

2. Visit the library

Next, spend an hour or two in the public library and read up on the company and the industry in general. Check the periodical indexes for articles in magazines and newspapers. If the company is large enough or is a publicly held corporation, you may also find good data in business reference books such as *Standard and Poor's Register of Corporations, Directors and Executives* and *Dun and Bradstreet's Million Dollar Directory.*

If you're not sure where to begin, don't be shy about asking the reference librarian for help. Even though I'm an old hand at doing library research, I always seek guidance from the librarians—they know the best and fastest ways to find information.

If you live near a college or university, visit its career center or placement office, too. These resource centers often are gold mines of information, and they generally are open to the public as well as to students.

3. Call your networking contacts

Try to talk to people who are familiar with the company. Call your friends and networking contacts, and ask if they know anyone who works for or does business with the company. When you turn up a good lead, call that person, introduce yourself and ask for a few minutes to chat about the company. Then ask the same kind of questions you would ask in an information interview (see Chapter 3 for a refresher).

This personal research is invaluable because you often learn things about the company that you'd never find in a published article or annual report. Sometimes, you can even get the low-down on the people who will be interviewing you—their likes and dislikes, communication styles, management styles, etc.

However, if you don't know the contact well, I wouldn't press for detailed information about specific interviewers. You don't want your contact to bump into the interviewer and say, "This person you're interviewing tomorrow called and asked all sorts of questions about you." If the contact volunteers the information without your asking for it, fine. Use it to your advantage.

4. Talk to your recruiter

Finally, if a search firm or employment agency arranged the interview for you, the recruiter should be able to fill you in on the company and the interviewer. But don't use this as your sole source of information; do your own detective work as well. You may or may not be hearing the full story from the recruiter. It's possible that the employer wasn't entirely forthcoming in providing information to the recruiting firm, and it's also possible that the recruiting firm hasn't been entirely forthcoming with you.

Step 2: Research the position

In addition to researching the company, you also need to find out as much as you can about the job itself. Why is the job available? Is it a new position? If not, why did the person who had the job leave? What are some of the problems you would be expected to solve if you were hired? What are the politics of the position? What is the career path for people in this position? Do they usually move up the ladder or stay put?

Unless you're going after a high-ranking executive position, it's unlikely that you'll find any of this information in library resources. Fortune magazine might do a story about the departure of the CEO of a major international corporation, but they'll probably pass on anything less sensational.

Where then, do you dig up this information? Again, if you're working with a search or employment firm, you can ask your recruiter.

Also check the annual reports and other materials you obtained from the company. These pieces sometimes contain organizational charts and brief descriptions of departments and jobs.

Networking contacts are another good resource. In some industries (and in some cities), everyone in town knows who left what job and why. As long as you remember that a certain percentage of what you hear is probably nothing more than rumor, this is often the best way to get a good fix on the job.

Step 3: Find out what you're worth

One of the biggest—and costliest—mistakes you can make is to go into your interviews without any idea of what the position should pay. It's likely that the interviewer will bring up this topic at some point during your first or second interview, and how you respond can have a big impact on whether you're considered for the job. It can also affect the outcome of your salary negotiations if you do get a job offer.

Later chapters explain in detail certain strategies you can use to answer salary questions and position yourself for a bigger paycheck. But you won't be able to use any of those strategies unless you have one key piece of information: the market value of the job and of your skills. You must determine the high, low and average salaries employers are paying for similar positions and for people with your level of experience.

You can find this information in several places. Professional trade organizations and business magazines, for example, publish annual salary surveys. Typically, these reports provide a breakdown of salaries by position, by level of experience and by geographic region. To find a salary survey that covers your field, ask a librarian for help or call the local branch of the appropriate trade organization for your field.

The government publishes salary data as well. Ask your librarian to help you find Department of Labor publications that might contain the data you need. Also look through career-planning guidebooks, which often include salary information for specific types of jobs.

When you're doing this research, be sure to look at salary figures for your geographic region. If you live in New York City, don't go by salary data for rural Tennessee—the local cost of living is an important factor in compensation levels. Your goal is to find out the going rate in your neck of the woods.

Be careful, too, to notice whether the figures you see are broken down by gender. If there's a discrepancy between male and female earnings, go by the highest figures. You should expect to be paid as much as people with your same level of experience, ability and education, regardless of gender.

Is all of this really necessary?

Absolutely, unequivocally, yes.

You say you're really busy and you don't have time to go to all of this trouble? Fine—just don't expect employers to have much time for you. They'll know from the moment you start talking that you don't have a good understanding of their problems and needs. If they do overlook that sore spot and offer you the job, you'll probably suffer in salary negotiations, because you won't know what's a fair price for your services and what's not.

It shouldn't take you more than a few hours in the library and on the phone to complete your pre-interview research. That's time well-spent for such a large payoff.

Chapter 11

Interview research: Part 2

Now that you have completed your company, job and salary research, you need to focus your investigative efforts in a new direction. This time, you're the subject.

Before you can determine the best way to present your qualifications in your interview, you must do a little self-study and figure out exactly what it is you're selling. What benefits will the employer gain by hiring you? What accomplishments in your past offer proof of your abilities? What special skills and unique talents can you bring to the job that others can't?

In this chapter, you'll complete a series of exercises that guide you through this important self-analysis. You'll also begin to plot your interview strategy and prepare your professional and personal references.

Step 1: Create a skills inventory

Get out your resume, if you have one, and the notes you took while conducting your research on the employer, position and salary. If you have any performance reviews from your current or past jobs, grab them, too, along with some blank paper and a pencil. Then head for a quiet room where you can work uninterrupted for an hour or so.

Your first task is to compile a written inventory of your skills. On a blank sheet of paper, list all of the major skills you offer the employer. For example:

- Computer skills
- Bookkeeping skills
- Organizational skills
- Communication skills
- Marketing skills

Leave about five or six lines of blank space between each major skill category.

Next, list the specific skills you offer in each category, noting how many years of experience you have in each area. For example:

- Computer skills
  WordPerfect   3 years
  Lotus 1-2-3   1 year

- Bookkeeping skills
  tax accounting   2 years
  wage statement preparation   2 years
  accounts payable/billing   1 year

If you've been out of the work force for a while or if this is your first foray into the working world, you may find it difficult to come up with a list of skills. Let me assure you that you do, in fact, have plenty of skills to offer. You simply need to look for them.

Suppose you've been a stay-at-home mom for the past four years. Think about the volunteer activities you participated in during those four years. Did you chair a fundraising drive for the PTA, for example? If you did, you probably used communication skills (you communicated with other members of the organization); marketing skills (you sold the group to would-be contributors); and leadership skills (you rounded up all the volunteers and made sure that everyone did what they were supposed to do).

Don't belittle this type of experience. As a volunteer, you use the very same skills you would use in a paid position. It's usually even tougher to succeed, because you're generally working with a very small budget and an unpaid labor force.

Consider, too, those tasks you did around the home. For instance, if you did the family budget, prepared your tax returns, bought a house or arranged a mortgage, you used accounting skills, planning skills and negotiating skills.

If you're just graduating from school, ask yourself what skills you used in your classes and social activities. If you held down a part-time job and managed to graduate with a decent grade point average, you definitely used organizational skills. If you were the treasurer of your sorority or photography club, you used financial and accounting skills.

I know what you're thinking—will employers really take that kind of experience seriously? The answer is yes, if you present it correctly. You must describe this experience in businesslike terms, and you must reinforce your words with a confidence level and appearance that says, "I may be new to the paid work force, but that doesn't mean I don't know how to be businesslike and professional."

Step 2: Rank your skills

If you've been a working woman for many years or very active in the volunteer world, the list of skills you compiled in Step 1 might be pretty extensive. Given the length of the typical interview—30 minutes to an hour—you'll probably run into trouble if you try to tell the interviewer about all the skills on your list. You won't be able to cover them in the kind of detail required to make a true sales impact. It's also likely that not all of the skills on your list are terribly relevant to the job opening, so it's a waste of time to focus on them during your interview. You're better off to narrow down your list and spend your interview time selling your top eight or 10 qualifications for the job. This allows you to explain in greater depth how those skills will benefit the company.

To determine which of your qualifications to emphasize, you must climb into the mind of your interviewers. Here's where your company and job research comes in handy. By reviewing it, you can get a good idea about what problems the employer is trying to solve and what skills are most needed to solve those problems. Those are the skills you should showcase in your interview.

So, taking what you know about the company, the interviewer and the position, rank the skills on your self-inventory list from most important to least important. Voilá! You have just determined your basic interview strategy. You'll spend the majority of your interview time selling the skills ranked highest on your list.

Step 3: Write down your accomplishments

It's not enough to simply claim that you have certain abilities or skills. You must prove it by describing specific accomplishments related to those skills.

For each of the 10 highest-ranked skills you listed in your skills inventory, jot down one or two related accomplishments. Explain not only what you did, but how your actions improved the bottom line of the company or organization. (For a review of how to present your accomplishments, reread Chapter 6.)

Here's an example to get you started:

Leadership skills

Accomplishment: I chaired the fundraising committee for the Bethesda junior high PTA for the last two years. Under my direction, the committee raised 25 percent more in revenue than the previous committee. Also, I was able to persuade all five committee members to commit to a two-year term on the committee. Before, the standard term anyone would agree to serve was one year, and people often quit the committee after only a few months.

Why I handled the project in this way: I made the two-year term commitment a priority because every time the committee members changed, we wasted time getting the new people up to speed. We also lost some valuable contacts in the community. I talked privately with each of the committee members to see what would motivate them to commit to a two-year term. All said that time considerations were the biggest factor in their decision. So I proposed that we limit our meetings to two hours each month, and they all agreed to stay on the committee for two years under that guideline. We then proposed the idea of a two-year term to the general membership, which approved it.

If you get stuck coming up with accomplishments, refer to your resume (by the way, you should include accomplishments on your resume, too) and to your old performance reviews. Also think about specific tasks or projects you completed as part of your student or volunteer activities. If you have an abundance of accomplishments, choose those that are most recent and most related to the position for which you're interviewing.

Step 4: Write down behavioral examples

In Chapter 5, you learned that many employers today are asking behavioral interview questions in addition to questions about specific technical skills. Behavioral questions usually focus on your "soft skills"—those aspects of your personality that enable you to work well with others and survive tough situations.

For each of the soft skills in the following list, describe a time when you used the skill to accomplish a goal. (You can skip any skills you already profiled in Step 3.) Be sure to include a brief statement explaining why you chose the course of action you did. Also, keep your answers work-related. Focus on a professional dilemma (or one you faced in a volunteer capacity), not on your personal trials and tribulations. Keep in mind that what the interviewer really wants to hear about are those skills that will help you succeed on the job.

- Leadership skills
- Stress-management skills
- Motivational skills
- Team-building skills
- Persistence
- Mediation skills
- Diplomacy skills
- Problem-solving and planning skills

Step 5: Anticipate objections

Next, play devil's advocate a bit. What objections might the employer have to hiring you? Do you lack a skill that the employer might think is vital? Was all of your experience gained in another, unrelated industry? Are you older or younger, more or less experienced than the rest of the staff? For each possible objection, write down a compensating skill or qualification. For example:

> Objection: *"You don't have experience working with our word-processing software."*
>
> Response: *"That's true. However, it's been my experience that most word-processing packages are quite similar, so I should be able to become proficient quickly. On my last job, I was able to make the transition to a new word-processing program in just two weeks."*

> Objection: *"We'd really like to have someone who's familiar with the food wholesaling business."*
>
> Response: *"It's true that I'm a newcomer to this industry. But from what you tell me about this job, the same skills that enabled me to be successful in my last position would enable me to be a super performer for you. For example, you need someone to break into the Southern sales region. In my current job, I opened up a new territory and delivered 125 percent of quota the first year."*

> Objection: *"You're overqualified for this job."*
>
> Response: *"It's true that I may have more experience than other applicants. But that additional experience will help me deliver better results for you."* (Note: This particular objection has many different facets, which are discussed more in Chapter 12.)

A word of caution: Don't go overboard with this exercise. The idea is not to beat yourself up or to focus on your shortcomings. The idea is simply that if you figure out ahead of time what objections might be raised, you can usually come up with a way to dodge them—presuming, of course, that you're reasonably well-qualified for the job. If you're not, it may be time to look for something more in line with your qualifications.

Step 6: Prepare your references

Almost every employer today requires job candidates to provide the names of people who can vouch for them on a personal and professional basis. Some companies don't ask you to provide these references unless you become one of the top candidates for the job, but others ask for them during the first interview, so you should always go prepared.

First, develop a list of at least three people who can attest to your professional abilities. Your references might include current and former managers, co-workers, clients or other business associates who are familiar with your qualifications and on-the-job performance. (If you don't want your current employer to know you're job hunting, don't use a fellow employee as a reference. Even the most trusted co-worker might slip up accidentally and let your secret out of the bag, which could prove embarrassing at best and job-threatening at worst.)

If you haven't held a paid job, list contacts from volunteer activities as references. If you're going after a secretarial position, for example, and you handled correspondence for your church group or PTA, give the name of a board member or officer who is aware of your correspondence skills.

You'll also need a few personal references. These are people who know you on a personal level and can testify to your high moral fiber and great personality. Ideally, your personal references should come from individuals who are known and respected in the community or, at the very least, known and respected by the employer. Don't list your Aunt Sally or your father as a personal reference. Employers assume that the opinions of relatives are not objective ones.

After compiling your lists, call your potential references. Ask whether they're willing to provide a reference, and if they agree, verify that you have their current job title, company affiliation and address. Then coach them a little. Describe the position you're seeking and tell them which skills are most important to the employer. Ask them to focus on those skills if possible when the employer calls for a reference check.

Be aware, too, that when employers call the references you've listed, they'll probably ask for the names of other people who might be able to provide insights into your abilities or personality. So give each of your references a list of suggested secondary references to mention. Be sure to also call and prepare those secondary references.

When you have a firm list of primary references, type it up or print it out on a high-quality computer printer. Include the full name, job title, company, address and phone number for each reference. It's also a nice touch to send a letter to your references and tell them how much you appreciate their offer to put in a good word for you.

Don't skip these steps!

If your schedule is as hectic as mine, I imagine that you're sorely tempted to skip all of this preparation and just "wing it" during your interview. I cannot urge you strongly enough to resist that temptation.

Remember what's at stake, and trust me when I tell you that if you invest the time it takes to work through these steps, you will reap benefits that far outweigh your effort. You'll not only be able to answer and ask interview questions in a much more powerful manner, but you'll gain the self-confidence that comes with understanding just how much you have to bring to the job.

Chapter 12

Sample interview questions

Ask a roomful of hiring managers and personnel specialists to write down their five favorite interview questions, and chances are good that no two lists will be the same. Every interviewer seems to have unique ideas about the best way to extract information from job candidates. You simply cannot predict exactly what questions you'll be asked in your interview.

However, you can make an educated guess about the interviewer's possible topics of inquiry. From your company research, you know what problems the company is facing, and it's likely that many questions will concern those issues. You also can assume that the interviewer will ask about your work habits and your attitudes toward industry issues, because most employers today are concerned about "corporate fit" as much as technical skills and abilities.

You should be able to discuss all of these subjects in your interview. You're already fairly well-prepared to do so, because you've done the appropriate background research and analyzed your skills and accomplishments. But you can prepare yourself even further by answering some actual interview questions. To that end, this chapter presents a list of sample questions plus some tips on how to respond to them.

After you read the background information on each question, draft your own answer, based on your skills and everything you have learned about the employer and the job. Some questions should be relatively easy for you to answer, because they relate to the research you did in previous chapters. Others require you to do a bit more analysis about your strengths, weaknesses, interests and goals.

The list of sample questions includes some behavioral-style interview questions and some of the stickier questions you may encounter, such as inquiries about your family status or salary expectations. It also includes some of the traditional favorites—those famous interview questions that have been around for years. Many interviewers today shy away from these moldy-oldies, but some interviewers do still ask them, especially those who are new to interviewing. More importantly, these questions (and the others in the list, too) provide good practice material because they give you a chance to focus on the topics that most interviewers address in some fashion or another. The experience you gain in putting your "features and benefits" into words will be invaluable in your interviews, even if you're not asked these specific questions.

How to answer the sample questions

Write down each question and your answer to it on a sheet of paper. When you finish drafting your initial answers, review and edit them until you're satisfied that they're as strong as they can be. (You'll need these notes to complete the remaining preparation exercises in Chapter 15, so don't skip this step.) Finally, run through the questions a second time, this time answering out loud and using your notes to guide you.

When you're answering the sample questions, refer to the following list, which summarizes strategies discussed in earlier chapters:

- Concentrate on the employer's needs, not yours.
- Emphasize how you can help the company achieve its goals.
- Focus on the bottom line.

- Describe accomplishments instead of simply reciting your past responsibilities.
- Explain why you approached the project a certain way.
- Explain how the skills you bring will benefit the company (sell benefits, not just features.)
- Use strong, confident language. (Review Chapter 9 for a refresher.)
- Don't downplay your accomplishments or attribute them to luck.

Questions about your skills and experience

"Tell me about yourself."

Vague, open-ended questions such as this one, which is often used by inexperienced interviewers to kick off the interview, can get you in a lot of trouble. If you're not careful, you can end up telling interviewers more—or less—than they want to know.

Different interviewers ask this question (or a variation of it) for different reasons. One hiring manager may want to know about your current position, for example. Another may want to hear about your entire work history, starting with your very first job. Yet another may be interested in finding out about your personality and approach to business. It's important that you address the interviewer's real concern, so clarify the question by asking, "What aspects of my background are you specifically interested in hearing about?"

For this exercise, draft answers for all three of the preceding scenarios. Always emphasize those experiences or traits that best sell you as the solution to the interviewer's problem. Focus on the skills you ranked as most important in your skills inventory. Suppose, for example, that you're interviewing for a job as a buyer in a department store. You have three years of experience as a retail-store manager, a degree in elementary education and four years experience as a childcare provider. From your company research, you know that the store is having problems because of poor relationships with suppliers. If the interviewer asks you to detail your current position, don't waste valuable interview time talking about your degree or your childcare experience—they're irrelevant. Instead, talk up the vendor-relations experience and skills you gained as a store manager.

Tip: Be careful not to ramble on when you're asked an open-ended question such as "Tell me about yourself." Even if interviewers say they want to hear the story of your life, make it a capsulized version. Many candidates, especially women, get carried away and launch into a 10- or 15-minute discourse. Keep your answers short and to the point, remembering that the point always is, "What you can do for the company?"

"What are your strengths and weaknesses?"

Interviewers ask this question not just to learn about your abilities and shortcomings, but to find out how you see yourself—to see whether you think you've got what it takes to do the job.

Obviously, you want to identify as your strengths those skills or personality traits that seem most vital to the position. But what about that weaknesses bit? Do you really want to admit that you're lacking in some area? The answer is yes— and no. Don't say that you don't have any weaknesses; employers are extremely suspect of people who give that response. As one hiring manager put it: "We all have weaknesses. And if you can't identify your weaknesses, you're going to have trouble down the road. Those weaknesses are going to show up, and you won't have given any thought to how to overcome them."

The key is to pick a weakness that: a) is low on the employer's list of required skills; and b) you're taking steps to correct. If you're applying for a managerial position, don't answer that your weakness is not being able to handle personnel conflicts well, for example. Better to mention your discomfort about having to speak to large groups and emphasize that you're going to your local Toastmasters Club to improve your skills.

Tip: Women, because of a tendency toward self-deprecation, often spend so much time explaining their weaknesses that they talk themselves out of a job. Mention one or two weaknesses and explain how you are overcoming them. Then quickly shift the focus and start selling your strengths.

"Tell me about some of your accomplishments."

If you've done your homework correctly, this should be an easy one. Simply describe the accomplishments from your self-inventory list that are most relevant to the job. Don't forget to stress your contribution to the bottom line and to explain why you approached the challenge or situation as you did. You need to show that you know how to assess a situation and plan a successful course of action.

In addition, don't dismiss your accomplishments as unimportant or attribute them to luck—a bad habit shared by too many women. Instead, say something like, "It took a lot of hard work, but I learned a lot from it, and it made a real impact on the company." An interview is not the place to downplay your abilities.

Be sure to describe any circumstances that made it more difficult for you to achieve your goal. For example, if you managed a department that met its sales quota during a period when your best producer was in the hospital, mention that and explain how you motivated the rest of the staff to pick up the slack. Often, what seems like a minor accomplishment at first glance is really a major achievement when you understand the circumstances under which it occured.

Tip: Don't try to win interviewers' favor by sharing information that your current or former employers consider confidential, especially if you're interviewing with a competing company. Interviewers will wonder whether you'd be just as forthcoming with their company secrets.

You can explain your bottom-line impact without giving specific numbers. For example, instead of saying that the average sales division in your company earned $1.2 million in sales revenue in the past year and your division earned $1,560,280, you can just say that your division outpaced the others by approximately 30 percent.

"Tell me about a significant failure."

When you answer this question, it's important to take responsibility for the failure and also to explain what you learned from it. Interviewers want to know if you understand why you failed and know how to avoid similar problems in the future. You should also explain why you think the failure was significant. Doing so reflects an understanding of what's important in business and what's not.

Resist the urge to cite a poor economy, an idiot boss or miserable co-workers as the reason for your failure. Employers don't respect people who blame others for their troubles. They do respect people who have the courage to say, "I blew it, and here's why it will never happen again."

Be careful not to let the discussion of your failure become too lengthy. You don't want to spend all of your interview time talking about your bad experiences. Women, in particular, often overplay their failures and downplay their successes. Keep your answer brief and move quickly to a more positive subject.

Tip: Try to follow up your failure story with an accomplishment that proves you learned your lesson.

"Tell me about a time when you..."

Interviewers often use this behavioral-style question to determine your soft skills. Typical endings to the "Tell me about a time when you..." opening are:

- Used leadership skills to accomplish a goal.
- Overcame a difficult situation.
- Dealt successfully with a stressful situation.
- Worked successfully in a team environment.
- Resolved a disagreement with a boss or co-worker.
- Took a risk to solve a problem.
- Motivated others to perform better.

Draft answers for each of these "Tell me about a time" questions. Again, you should be well-prepared if you did the exercises in Chapter 11. Keep in mind that the more you can describe the experience—the people involved, the challenge and your solution—the more you'll stand out in the interviewer's mind. Don't simply say, "I led a committee that acquired funding for a historical preservation project." Instead, create a specific, memorable image that makes it easier for the interviewer to remember you. For example:

"I led a committee that acquired funding to pre-serve a historic building in my neighborhood. It was a stop on the Underground Railroad during the Civil War, and it had fallen into such disrepair that the city was close to condemning the property. It was a difficult task, because the committee was comprised of people with several different interests. For example, one person wanted to turn the building into a for-profit museum, and another one wanted to donate it to the Urban League. Every time we tried to complete the proposal to the city, we got bogged down in long debates about how the building would be used.

I knew that if we got sidetracked over plans for the building, we stood a big risk of losing it altogether, be-cause the city wanted to move quickly one way or the other. I was able to convince everyone that we should put aside our different opinions on the use of the build-ing for the time being and concentrate on saving the structure. They agreed to do so, and we were able to get the proposal completed and approved quickly after that."

A story such as this gives the interviewer a more vivid record of your accomplishments and skills. This technique—which, by the way, applies to other questions as well—is espe-cially valuable when the employer is interviewing many can-didates in a short span of time.

Tip: It's important not to make negative statements about the people in your examples. Don't say, "Oh, I had big disagree-ments with my boss on a lot of issues, because he was a real jerk," or "Well, I certainly had to deal with a lot of stress on my last job. That place was a real zoo." You goal here is to demon-strate your political savvy and your ability to work well with others, even if they're jerks.

Questions about your personality and goals

"Why do you want to work here?"

Interviewers ask this question to assess several things. First, they want to find out how much you know about the company. They also want to learn about your motivation. Do you want this particular job because of money? Because you heard that the company was a great place to work? Because you think you would enjoy the day-to-day responsibilities? Because you can't stand where you're at now and think any job would be an improvement?

Your goal is to assure the interviewer that you're not just after any old job but that you chose this particular job and company because you think you can really contribute. You should also demonstrate that you've given careful thought to your career goals, because employers appreciate focused individuals.

If you were applying for a job as a research chemist at a drug company, for example, you might answer as follows:

> *"I've been doing a lot of research on different companies, and I believe that your company not only offers the right corporate culture for me, but that the position is a good fit for me, too. I'm interested in gaining solid experience in research, and Steel Drugs is one of the best places to get that experience. As for this particular position, it appeals to me because I want to spend my working hours making a difference; accomplishing things gives me a sense of satisfaction. And I think that my skills and experience will enable me to be a producer for you."*

Don't be phony or overly gushing—you don't have to say, "I think you're the very best company in the world and I don't want to work for anyone but you." But do let the interviewer know that you are excited about the possibility of being part of the organization. It's also important to include some benefits for the employer in this statement, so that your response isn't all "me-oriented." The last sentence in the preceding example accomplishes this and provides a neat segue to a discussion of your specific skills.

If you're a displaced homemaker or are returning to the work force after raising a family, you may also have to answer a variation of the "Why do you want to work here" question. The interviewer may want to know why you want to work, period. This question usually is a sign that the interviewer thinks you may not be serious about a career. Your answer should assure the interviewer that your decision to work is not a whim, but a carefully researched and planned life goal. (If this situation applies to you, draft a response on your practice answer sheet.)

Tip: A major gripe among employers is that many applicants, especially those who are relatively new to the work force, have unrealistic expectations about work. These "work fantasies" often show up when the candidates answer the "why do you want to work here" question.

I witnessed this tendency first-hand during my stint as associate editor for a travel magazine. Many applicants sat in my office and said they wanted to join the staff because the idea of working for a magazine sounded so glamorous and exciting. I generally passed on people who saw the job in that light. I knew that they'd be sorely disappointed once they found out the truth: The job entailed a lot of long, grueling hours of research and solitary writing work—hardly the dazzling lifestyle they imagined.

The moral of that little story is that it's a good idea to let the employer know that although you're really enthusiastic about the job, you also understand that work is just that—work. You might even say something like:

> "I know how hard a job like this can be. I'm familiar with the long hours and effort that it requires to be successful. But I also think that it would be very rewarding and exciting."

"Why are you leaving your current job?"

Interviewers who ask this question want to know if you're leaving because you've been unable to succeed or fit in at your current company. They quite naturally assume that if you have problems at your present company, you'll have problems at their company. They also may be interested in determining whether any of the issues that prompted you to leave your present position—salary, advancement opportunities, working conditions—exist in their company as well. If those issues do exist, they probably will eliminate you from further consideration, because they figure that you'll be just as unhappy in your new job as you were in your old one.

The best approach is to explain that you're running toward a new opportunity, not running away from a bad situation. For example, you can simply say something to the effect of:

"I've been successful at the Phillips Company, but I'm ready for a new challenge. I'm looking outside the company because the opportunities for those new challenges simply aren't readily available in-house."

Tip: Whatever you do, don't badmouth your current company; it shows a lack of respect for and loyalty to your employer. If you're leaving because the company hasn't been doing very well and you're afraid you'll be laid off, don't bring that up, either. For one thing, the information may not be widely known, and if you reveal it, the interviewer may see you as someone who blabs company secrets. Additionally, if employers are aware that your current job situation is shaky, they have an edge in salary negotiation. They may offer you less, knowing that you may be desperate to get a job.

"What are your career goals?"

Interviewers who ask this question do so not because they care so much about your personal happiness, but because they want to know whether you're likely to stay with the company for a while. They also want to know whether you really are interested in the job that's available or see it as an fast springboard to something better. Unless the company is actively looking for people they can move up quickly through the ranks, announcing that you want to be promoted within 12 months is a death wish. With the high cost of training and hiring employees today, interviewers are likely to cut you from the running if they think you won't be happy in the job for a reasonable amount of time.

It's also important to show that you're flexible, so when you answer this question, find a middle ground between having no goals at all and having your life planned out down to the finest detail, all the way to retirement. You want to show that you do have some goals that are important to you and that the job in question fits nicely with those goals. You also need to stress that your goals aren't written in stone—that you're always open to new opportunities. Here's an example:

"Well, this job meets my immediate goal, which is to find an opportunity where I can gain experience and yet be an active producer in the marketing field. It's difficult to look into a crystal ball and tell you exactly where I think I'll be in five or 10 years, but in general terms, I'll seek out the opportunity to assume more responsibility as I grow and prove my abilities to you. If the chance to move into marketing management opens up, I'd be interested in pursuing that, but I'm also open to exploring other areas of the business, too—for example, operations."

Tip: Remember that many interviewers believe the stereotype that women are less interested in a long-term career and worry that a woman will leave the company after a short time to raise children. You might want to emphasize that you're in it for the long haul by adding to your goal statement something like, "I plan to continue building my career, because that is a priority in my life."

"What is your management style?"

If you're interviewing for a supervisory position, you'll no doubt hear this question. The interviewer wants to know if your approach to management fits the type of people you'll be supervising and the overall corporate management style. As always, you should try to pin interviewers down a bit more so that you can be sure what management issues they're most concerned about. Your motivational methods? Your ideas about fraternizing with the staff? Your technique for dealing with people who make mistakes? Ask a clarifying question, such as: "Well, management style encompasses a lot of issues, and I'd like to talk about those areas that are of most concern to you. What is the biggest management problem I'd be facing?"

To give yourself some practice answering questions about your management style, draft responses to three specific questions:

1. How do you motivate employees?
2. How do you discipline employees?
3. What is your idea of the ideal employee/boss relationship?

If your company research alerted you to other management questions the interviewer is likely to ask, create answers for those as well.

Tip: Many employers, as you know, believe the stereotype that women don't know how to wield management power. Most often, this is because our management styles are different than a man's. You may want to reinforce the notion that although your style may be different, you're no less effective. For example, you might say:

> "I often surprise people; they think that because I'm a woman I don't know how to be tough. It's true that I don't yell and scream or threaten—I believe using the team approach is more effective. And my performance record proves that you don't have to come across as a fire-eating bully to accomplish what you need to accomplish."

"What do you do in your spare time?"

This question is designed to help the interviewer assess your personality. Are you a workaholic, or do you have a good balance between your work and personal life? Are you someone who takes an active part in your community, or is your idea of community involvement limited to attending the local high school football games? If you are involved, do you participate in any activities that might prove embarrassing to the company?

You might think that the best answer to this question would be to say that you don't have any spare time because you work so hard at your job. Everybody wants a dedicated worker, right? Yes, to an extent. But employers today are also searching for well-balanced individuals who place equal importance on their personal and professional lives. They have learned that employees who spend 18 hours a day on the job very quickly burn out.

Just as you emphasize those skills and accomplishments that are most relevant to the position, mention those outside activities that are most likely to be positives in the interviewer's mind. Fitness activities are good bets because employers prefer healthy employees. Participation in professional trade groups is another winner because it shows that you have a keen interest in the industry. Volunteering in community activities also is a plus, but be careful: If you're a strident supporter of some political, religious or otherwise potentially controversial group, I wouldn't bring it up. The interviewer just may be a strident member of the opposition.

Tip: Here again, the more specific you can be, the better. Don't just say that you like to take part in community activities and play tennis. That's a gray visual image that's hard to remember. So give some details:

> *"I'm an active member of the Ambassador's Club, which is a group that provides volunteer services for a number of community events. For example, last year I served as a host and driver for one of the athletes during the NCAA Diving Competition. Also, I'm a tennis buff—I'm taking lessons over at Eagle Park and play in a city league."*

Questions about sticky issues

"Are you married? Do you have children?"

The law forbids employers from basing hiring decisions on your marital or family status. That doesn't stop most employers from asking about these issues. You don't have to answer, of course. But where will that get you? Out the door, most likely. Let's say that the employer does mean to discriminate. If you refuse to answer, the interviewer will assume that you're "one of those women's libbers" or that you won't answer because you do in fact have family conflicts that might hinder your job performance. Either way, your defiance will be a big black mark against you.

Now let's suppose that your interviewers are simply ignorant of the law. Should you enlighten them? Well, if you did, my guess is that they would either become embarrassed or defensive—and neither emotion is conducive to building your interview rapport.

It's no secret that many employers believe that women who are wives and mothers miss work frequently, are reluctant to travel and often quit to follow their husbands to a new job location. So if you are a wife or a mother or both, how do you answer questions about your family status without damaging your chances for the job? By keeping the employer's true concerns in mind.

Questions about your family life really represent a hidden objection. The interviewer doesn't really care that you have a loving husband or that you've chosen to have children. The issue is whether your lifestyle will affect your ability to do the job in any way. Which means that the best way to answer such questions is to say something on the order of the following:

> *"Yes, I do have two children. I have great childcare arrangements, too, so you don't have to worry that my family might interfere with my work. We even have a backup plan in place so that if our regular caregiver is sick, I don't have to miss work to be with the kids."*

or:

> *"Yes, I do have a family, but I make it a point not to let that interfere with my work. In fact, at my last job, I never missed one day because of family problems or sick children."*

Recognize the employer's fear and offer a brief statement that calms those fears. Don't belabor the point, and don't let the interviewer get sidetracked into a discussion of family issues or stories about childcare or schooling. As quickly as you can, direct the interviewer's attention to a new topic by asking a question about the specific duties of the job or the company.

If the interviewer really starts to focus on your personal life, you can usually put a halt to it with a simple statement such as:

> *"You know, I sense that you're concerned about whether my personal life will keep me from performing well. I can assure you that this has not been the case in the past and it won't be so in the future.*

This same approach is effective when interviewers ask other types of discriminatory questions, too. Just for the record, the law restricts employers from basing hiring decisions on your age, ancestry or race, as well as on many aspects of your personal life, including your religion and your sexual orientation.

Tip: As irritating and infuriating as these questions can be, don't let your feelings show. This is not the place to mount your own personal war against discrimination, unless you really, really don't want the job. Smile, deliver your answer in a polite, professional tone and then shut up and look expectantly at the interviewer, as if to say, "Next question?"

"You're overqualified. Why do you want this job?"

Like the preceding question, this question is really a hidden objection. But the statement "you're overqualified" can reflect many different objections. One interviewer may be afraid that you'll want too much money. Another might worry that you'll be bored on the job. Yet another might be concerned that as soon as a better offer comes along, you'll be gone.

Before you can answer, you must find out the interviewer's true objection. You can say something like:

> *"I realize that I may be more qualified than some of the other applicants for this job. But I truly am interested in this position, so will you tell me what specific concerns you have about my experience level so that I can relieve you of those worries?"*

After you learn the interviewer's major objection, you can address it. Explain honestly why you believe the job is right for you and is not a step down but a step that's in line with your career goals. More importantly, remind the interviewer of the additional benefits the company will gain because of your added experience.

As before, prepare yourself to answer this question by drafting responses for each of the three scenarios described:

- The interviewer thinks you want too much money.
- The interviewer thinks you'll be bored.
- The interviewer thinks you'll quit as soon as you get a better offer.

Tip: Sometimes, "you're overqualified" is another way of saying, "I think you might be too old." If you sense this may be the case—for example, if everyone in the company is in their mid-20s and you're in your 50s—play up your ability to deal with co-workers of all ages and your knowledge of the latest industry theories and technology. You need to reassure the interviewer that you'll fit in with the gang and also that "older" doesn't mean "outdated."

"Why have you changed jobs so often?"

If you've been a job-hopper, you'll probably be asked to explain it in your interviews. The best response is simply to say that it's taken you a while to find the right career path, but that you believe you're on that path now. You should never say something like, "Well, I've had a lot of crummy jobs and I just always got fed up and quit." You must convince the interviewer that you're not going to go hopping off to some other job three or four months after you're hired.

If you have an erratic work history because of some other circumstance that no longer exists—an ex-husband's frequent job relocation, for example—it's important to stress that fact.

Tip: For you, it's doubly important to emphasize your accomplishments in the interview. You need to make it clear that although you only stayed at each job for a short time, you contributed to each company during your brief stay. You can also "accentuate the positive" by pointing out that because you've been exposed to a lot of different companies, you have experience working with many different types of people and in many different environments.

"Were you ever fired or laid off?"

If you've been fired, you're probably terrified that the subject will come up in your interview. Don't be. Most employers say that unless the candidate has been fired over and over again, they don't pay much attention to this information. And of course, in today's economy, being laid off is hardly the disgrace it once was—employers know that layoffs often have nothing to do with performance.

You do need to be careful, however, in how you present this information. Don't get defensive; understand that the interviewer's question is not a personal attack. If you were fired, be honest about what happened, without going into all the gory details. It's best to use the same approach recommended for answering questions about your failures: "I made a mistake, and I learned a valuable lesson from it."

If you were laid off, try to emphasize that your dismissal was unrelated to your performance. You might say something like:

> *"Being laid off was especially frustrating because I was enjoying a lot of success in my job. I was able to reduce accounting expenses in our department by 20 percent, for example. But the company's business was such that a reduction in staff simply was unavoidable."*

If you've been out of work for a long time, be sure to stress that you've been actively using your skills nonetheless. Play up your volunteer activities or any professional retraining you've done. This shows that you're a motivated person, not someone who just sits around waiting for the phone to ring.

Tip: Never lie to interviewers about being fired or laid off—and for that matter, don't lie about your qualifications for the job, either. Sooner or later, you'll be found out, and you'll end up looking worse than if you had been honest. Keep in mind, too, that the interviewer may already know more about you than you think and may ask you certain questions just to gauge your integrity.

"How much do you make? How much do you want?"

This is very dangerous and potentially costly territory, so use extreme care in how you answer these two questions. Your answers set the stage for later salary negotiations and may even put you out of the running for the job.

If your salary expectations are much above or much below what the employer has in mind, it's likely that you won't be considered further. If your expectations are too high, the employer will assume that you won't be interested in the job.

If they're too low, the employer will assume that you either don't have a good understanding of what the job entails or that you don't have the skills necessary to command a fair market price.

Revealing your current salary also can kill any chances you have for obtaining a much higher salary than you're making at your present job. Although some employers say they don't consider an applicant's current salary when making a job offer, just as many others say they won't offer more than 10 or 15 percent above the current salary.

What's the solution? The best tactic is to put off any discussion of salary until they offer you the job. You can simply say:

> *"You know, money is important to me, but it's not the most important thing. I'm sure that if we both agree that this job is a good fit for me, we can come to an agreement."*

If the interviewer persists, answer by giving the salary range you determined during your job research. Always state a fairly broad range: "I understand that a fair market price for a position such as this is in the range of $25,000 to $38,000." Be sure that the bottom figure in your range reflects the minimum you're willing to take for the job.

Answering questions about your current salary are a bit stickier. To position yourself as well as possible for future salary negotiations, include the value of all benefits, perks and other compensation in the figure you give. If you are paid below market value on your current position, make it clear that you expect to be paid appropriately on your new job. For example:

> *"My total compensation package is worth $18,500— which is about $5,000 below market value. That's one reason why I'm looking for new opportunities."*

Tip: Interviewers look for obvious signs of discomfort when they ask this question. If you start fidgeting or display other nervous mannerisms when you address salary questions, it's a sure tip-off to the employer that you're not really sure what you're worth and that you don't much like talking about it. Saying too much about salary—going on and on about why you deserve this or that or otherwise talking the subject to death— is another signal that you're lacking confidence in your worth. So stay calm, look the interviewer in the eye, answer the question briefly and then be quiet. (More techniques for effective salary negotiation are covered in Chapters 17 and 18.)

Other sample questions

After you've written your answers to the preceding questions, draft your responses to the following additional questions about your skills, your personality and your goals. Remember to include specific accomplishments, focus on the bottom line and emphasize skills that are most relevant to the employer's needs.

- What extracurricular activities did you participate in during your high school and college years?
- Why did you choose this career?
- What are some of the challenges you're facing in your current job and what are you doing to overcome them?
- What do you enjoy about this line of work?
- What aspects of this position are most attractive/least attractive to you?
- What types of tasks do you enjoy the most?
- How do you feel about travel and/or relocation?
- What do you think it takes to succeed in business today?
- Do you prefer working alone or in a group?
- Tell me about a time when a superior criticized you. How did you react to that and what did you do afterward?
- Tell me about a time when you faced an ethical or moral dilemma and how you resolved it.
- How would your co-workers and your boss describe you?

- How do you define stress?
- What jobs have you enjoyed the most during your career? The least?
- What makes you different from all of the other people who applied for this job?
- How have you gotten along with your boss in previous jobs? With co-workers?
- How do you deal with co-workers who disagree with you?
- Do you have any objection to working overtime if it's required?
- What is the most difficult situation you've faced in your career, and how did you handle it?

After answering these questions, put yourself in the role of the employer for a minute. Are there any other questions you would ask if you were the employer? If you were interviewing someone who had a work history similar to yours? Try to anticipate any additional questions you may be asked and then develop answers for them as well. This is one time you can't be too well-prepared!

The next step

Drafting answers to possible interview questions is only half of your pre-interview preparation. You also must come up with a list of questions that you'll ask the interviewer. The next chapter gives you some advice on this very important aspect of the interview.

Chapter 13

How to interview the employer

A friend of mine—I'll call her Rebecca—took a new job as an executive assistant not too long ago. Soon after she accepted the job offer, she called to tell me about her good fortune. "I'm going to be the president's right-hand person!" she enthused.

After offering my congratulations, I asked what her job responsibilities would be. "That's sort of up in the air," she replied. "They don't have a firm job description yet because they plan to hire someone else to take on part of the work soon."

I then inquired whether she'd gotten the salary she wanted. "Well," she admitted, "the pay's a little low right now, but they promised to bump it up and add some benefits after I've been there a while. Evidently they're waiting for some compensation expert to finish reviewing their pay plan and then they're going to restructure everything. Oh, and they also said that if I do well, I can really move up quickly—maybe even to a director's position!"

Unfortunately, after about a week on the job, Rebecca discovered that the reality of her new position was very different from the picture she'd envisioned. A co-worker told her that the previous executive assistant quit because the workload was impossible—it turned out that the president had been promising to hire a second assistant for years. When Rebecca casually asked another employee about the timetable on the compensation study, he laughed and said, "Oh, you fell for that too! I've been waiting two years for my 'restructuring' to come through." As for the opportunity to advance into a director's position, it didn't take long for Rebecca to figure out that she had a better chance of being named Queen of England. A quick look at the organizational chart revealed that the highest-ranking woman in the company was a first-line supervisor, and she was the president's niece! The worst part of the whole thing was that Rebecca turned down two other offers to accept this job.

Rebecca got herself in this mess because she made a critical and very common mistake: She neglected to ask questions during her interviews. She didn't ask for specifics about the position. She didn't ask when the company planned to hire a second assistant or to complete the compensation study, and she didn't ask whether any women in the company had obtained executive rank. If she had, she probably would have gotten the clues she needed to determine that the job was going to be a nightmare. At the very least, she would have known to bargain for more money, given the circumstances of the position.

To preserve my journalistic integrity, I should confess at this point that Rebecca isn't a real person—rather, her tale is a composite of many similar horror stories I've heard from friends and acquaintances over the years. Some of those stories weren't quite as bad as this one, and some were a lot worse. Regardless, the moral is the same. If you don't interview your interviewers as carefully as they interview you, you can easily wind up in a lousy situation.

Don't wait for them to tell you

Employers want to attract the best talent they can find. Because they want to convince you that the company is a great place to work, they tend to describe job openings in the most positive light. Sometimes, employers are downright misleading, leaving out important details about the job or making glib promises they know will never be kept. More often, they simply forget or don't think it necessary to discuss certain aspects of the position or company that might prove important to your job satisfaction.

It's your responsibility to ask for the information you need to form an accurate and complete picture of the company and the job. You should make sure that you'll enjoy the job, that you have a reasonable chance of being successful in it and that the corporate culture suits your personal and professional style. If you accept a position that doesn't meet all of these criteria, you'll almost certainly be repeating your job-hunting chores before too long.

Many people are very uncomfortable with this aspect of the interview. They're afraid that they'll somehow anger or offend the interviewer if they ask a lot of questions. It's true that if you quiz interviewers in an overly aggressive or defensive tone of voice, badger them for proprietary information or ask inappropriate questions, you will offend and anger. But if you ask the right questions, in a friendly, professional manner, you not only won't turn interviewers off, you'll win points with them.

Employers actually favor candidates who ask questions during interviews. They know that employees who aren't happy about some aspect of the job or who don't fit in with the corporate culture usually are less productive workers. Such employees also tend to quit or get themselves fired shortly after they're hired. With the high cost of recruiting and training today, that's an expense employers simply can't afford. They realize that it's in their best interest to help you make sure that the job and company are right for you.

In addition, asking questions during the interview helps you get a clearer idea of the specific problems the employer is trying to solve. This information tells you which of your skills and experiences to emphasize most during your interview.

When to ask which questions

In some cases, the employer may conduct only one round of interviews before making a hiring decision, which means that you'll have to do all of your fact-finding during the first interview. You may want to ask up front how many interviews the employer will conduct before making a decision so that you can gear your questions accordingly. If you learn that candidates will go through two or more interviews, use the first interview for general information-gathering and then get more specific during each subsequent interview.

You may be interviewed by someone from HR as well as by the hiring manager. As you do with your interview answers, it's important to gear your questions to the interviewer. The HR person is best equipped to answer broad-based questions about corporate philosophy and culture, while the hiring manager can provide the most detailed information about the responsibilities and challenges of the job.

Questions about the job

The specific questions you ask will depend upon the nature of the interview, the position and your personal concerns. But in general, you need to make sure that you understand all of the daily tasks and responsibilities associated with the position. You also should know what short- and long-term goals you'll be expected to meet and under what conditions you'll have to meet them. In addition, you should find out where the position falls in the management structure and how your performance will be evaluated.

To discover this information, you can ask such questions as:

- May I see the job description for this position?
- What tasks will occupy the majority of my time?
- Can you describe a typical day on the job?
- Will I be working on most projects by myself or in a group?
- What are the three top goals you've set for this position for the coming year?
- Is this a newly created position, or am I replacing someone? Did the person who had the job before fail or succeed, and why?
- What are the biggest challenges I'll face in this position?
- To whom will I be reporting?

- Is there a training period?
- How will my performance be evaluated?
- How is successful performance rewarded?
- How much, if any, overtime is typically required in this position?
- How does this position fit in with the company's long-term plans?
- What is the typical career path for someone in this job?

If the position is a management job, you'll also want to ask such questions as:

- How many people will I be supervising?
- What is the operating budget I'll be handling?
- What is the experience level of the staff I will be managing?
- Will I have authority to assign duties, reward performance and discipline the staff, or will these issues be handled by my superiors?
- What is the preferred management style here?
- Are any staff increases or reductions planned for this department in the next few years?
- Does the company plan to expand this department in the future?
- Has the employee turnover rate in this department been higher than average/lower than average? Why?

Because your goal is to learn all you can about the job, ask whether you can talk with one or two people in the department, too. Discussions with the people who would be your peers or your staff often turn up information that the hiring manager or HR person may be reluctant to share. You also may learn about important benefits or interesting challenges that the interviewers forgot to mention.

When you talk to other staff members, ask them such questions as:

- What do you like and dislike about the job?
- What do you see as the biggest challenges of your job?
- What do you like and dislike about the company?

In addition, ask some of the same questions you asked the hiring manager and the HR interviewer. If you hear very different answers, it may be a sign that something's amiss. Granted, most employees won't risk their jobs by offering up all of the company dirt, but usually they'll tell you what you want to know in a roundabout way. For example, suppose the interviewer tells you that the company is about to add on some great new benefits. If those enhancements really aren't as imminent as the interviewer implies, staff members may not come right out and say, "That's a joke—they've been promising us that for years." But they may give you a tight-lipped smile and say something like, "Well, if I were you, I would base my decision on the current situation." It doesn't take a brain surgeon to figure out that you can probably discount any promises of future benefits.

One side note: Some companies hire women and minorities just to satisfy EEOC or public-image concerns. Given today's tight corporate budgets, this practice isn't that prevalent, but it does happen. If you have any suspicions at all that you might end up in a "token" position, where you would be in the spotlight a lot but wouldn't be given any real responsibilities, you can ask questions such as:

- How do you rank the contribution of this position on the company's bottom line—is it not very important or very important?
- How much, if at all, will I be involved in making policy or procedural decisions that affect my department or the company?

Questions such as these help you determine the real role the company has planned for you.

Questions about the company

Finding out about the corporate culture is every bit as important as getting details about the job. You need to take an objective look at the company's business philosophy, work environment and cultural attitudes. If you want to do well on the job, let alone enjoy your work, it's critical that you find an employer—and a boss—whose personality and professional attitudes are in sync with your own.

Why is this corporate fit so important? Because if you feel restrained or otherwise uncomfortable with the work environment or atmosphere, you'll be unhappy. You'll also find it hard to be effective or successful if you work or interact with others in a manner that varies greatly from the corporate norm.

"The key to success is being able to work within an environment where you're ultimately accepted and valued for what you do," explains Mary Jo Zaksas, who spent many years as a corporate recruiter and HR director before becoming president of Zaksas Associates, a Chicago-based retained search firm. "Don't think that you can change your direction to fit the corporate culture, because you're not going to be able to adjust that quickly," she adds. "Remaking yourself to fit someone else's style rarely has good results."

In addition to assessing the overall corporate culture, you must consider the culture in the specific department where you would be working. It's possible that the two are very different. For example, if the company is largely a laid-back, liberal organization but you would report to a department manager who is a devout member of a conservative religion, you might have to follow different rules of conduct and expression than if you worked for other company managers.

Among the questions you might want to ask about the company in general are:

- What is the company's management philosophy?
- What sort of person is likely to succeed here? What sort of person usually fails?
- What is the company's attitude about advancing people from within?
- How would you describe the overall work atmosphere?

- If I were to talk to the employees here, what would they tell me about the company?
- Does the company have a higher than average turnover rate? Why?
- What do your employees find most attractive and least attractive about working here?

When you interview with the person who will be your supervisor, you should ask such questions as:

- What is your management philosophy?
- Do you prefer that your staff members keep in close contact with you or work very independently?
- Why have the people who haven't been successful in your department failed? What sort of people have been successful?
- How would you describe your ideal employee?

If you're a woman who wants to advance in your career, it's vital to determine whether the corporate culture is female-friendly, too. At some point, you may want to ask to see the company's organizational chart—although such charts sometimes only show last names, so that may not tell you much. You also can review the company's annual report and count the number of women on the board of directors. Or, you can point-blank ask. You have to be subtle, though; you can't just say, "So, does this firm discriminate against women?" Any interviewer with half a brain will answer, "Absolutely not." Instead, try something to the effect of:

> *"I'm very serious about my career, and I do want to advance when I'm qualified to do so. So I'm curious about women who have been promoted to management positions here—what personal or professional characteristics did they display that enabled them to succeed?"*

If the company has a die-hard policy against women, you'll know pretty quickly, because the interviewer won't be able to describe any women who have advanced into management.

Closing questions

At the end of the interview, you need to ask two important questions. First, find out whether the interviewer has any concerns about your skills, experience or other qualifications. Say something like:

> "Based on what I've told you today, do you have any concerns about my ability to succeed in this job?"

Your goal is to turn up any hidden objections—concerns that the interviewer might not have voiced during your conversation. If the interviewer does mention an objection, present a skill or accomplishment that helps eliminate that objection. Sometimes, it's simply a matter of reminding the interviewer that you are skilled in a particular area. Other times, you may need to offer additional examples of experiences or accomplishments to prove your abilities. If you can't do so, describe other qualifications that make up for your lack of experience in the area of concern.

The second closing question actually is part statement, part question. As discussed in Chapter 6, "Sales 101," you should always conclude the interview by expressing your interest in the job and then asking when and how you can move forward in the hiring process. Here's an example of a good closing question:

> "I'm very enthusiastic about pursuing this position with you. When and how do we take the next step?"

It's also a good idea to ask the interviewer if you can call for an update if you don't hear from the company by the anticipated date. When you have the interviewer's permission to do so, you don't need to worry that you'll appear pushy if you call to inquire about the progress of the hiring decision.

What not to ask

Just as you can really impress interviewers by asking insightful, intelligent questions, you can create a negative image by asking the wrong questions.

It's a mistake, for example, to probe for specifics on benefits, perks, vacation time or raises or to focus too much on compensation during the interview process. Employers' main motivation is making a profit, and they expect your main motivation to be making them a profit, too—not making a profit for yourself.

Most experts advise that you shouldn't even inquire about salary until you receive a firm job offer. You're supposed to let the interviewer bring up the subject of compensation. I agree with this, but only to a certain extent. If you suspect that the salary level might be far below what you could accept, and you don't think that the employer will be interested in negotiating a higher salary, there's really not much point in going through two or three interviews until the employer gets around to talking about salary. And there's no guarantee that the employer will ever get around to stating the salary if you don't ask. That seems incredible, but several people I know received job offers from employers who never once said what the salary would be, even at the time the offer was made. Some of those employers said they wouldn't be able to determine salary until after the person was on the job for several months! It goes without saying that you should never, ever accept a job offer without a clear agreement on salary.

If, by the second interview, the interviewer hasn't stated a salary range for the job and you're concerned about the compensation level, you can say something like:

> "Compensation isn't my main concern at this point, but just to be sure that we're both in the same ballpark, what salary range do you have in mind for this position?"

After stating a salary range, the interviewer will probably ask whether that range suits your needs. If the salary is lower than you expected but you're still interested in the job—or you think you can talk the employer up to your range—you can make a statement such as:

> "As I said, money is not my main motivation at this point, and I'm sure that if we both decide that I'm right for this job, we can come to an agreement on salary. So why don't we set that issue aside for now and talk more about the job and how I might fit in here."

Of course, if the salary is much higher than you expected, simply say, "Yes, we're in the same neighborhood." Don't let on that you can't believe the salary is that high, or the interviewer will start to wonder why you might not be worth so much. (We'll talk more about how to handle this salary question and others in Chapter 18.)

In addition to asking detailed questions about compensation, asking too many questions about advancement opportunities is a bad move. You don't want to imply that you won't be happy doing this particular job for very long. And of course, don't ask about the company's policies on family leave or sick time during your interviews; you don't want to present yourself as someone who expects to need a lot of time off.

Look for the subtext

The answers that interviewers give to your questions aren't your only source of information. You can learn a lot about the company and the job simply by noticing what questions you're being asked and how the interviewer and other employees behave.

Let's say that you're a woman who's very interested in moving up the corporate ladder, for example. If the interviewer asks about your marital or family status, that should trigger a question in your mind about the company's attitudes toward women. Similarly, if an interviewer asks a lot of questions like, "How are you at dealing with stress," "How do you feel about overtime" and "How do you handle pressure," you can pretty much assume that the job involves long, hectic hours.

Pay attention to body language, too. If interviewers look uncomfortable or have a hard time looking you in the eye as they're responding to a question, it's a sign that they may not be telling you the whole truth.

In addition to observing the interviewer closely, keep your eyes and ears open as you walk through the company. Do the employees you see look like a happy bunch? Or is everybody rushing around in a frenzy, looking stressed and overworked? Do they look bored or animated? Are they wearing chinos and deck shoes or conservative suits and ties? Is the atmosphere relaxed or somber? You can pick up a great deal of information about the corporate culture from these outward signs.

To determine whether the company holds women in high regard, note the number of female names on the management-office doors and listen to the way male employees address their female co-workers. Do they speak to the women with courtesy and respect, or is there a lot of "Hey, honey" and "Darlin'" going on?

If possible, visit the company before the day of your interview with the specific purpose of assessing the environment. If you're interviewing for a job in a bank, for example, sit in the lobby for a while and observe the activity and the atmosphere. At the very least, arrive 15 or 20 minutes early for your interview. Tell the receptionist that you've arrived early for your appointment and you'd like to sit and gather your thoughts until the scheduled interview time; otherwise, you might be ushered into the interviewer's office right away and miss the chance to do this important detective work.

Don't take just any job

If you're desperate for a job, you may not think that it matters much whether the corporate culture and the position are truly appropriate for you. I want to emphasize again that if you take a job that's ill-suited for you, the chances are very good that you'll soon be back on the job-hunting trail. You'll not only have to go through all of this rigmarole again, but you'll have added a black mark to your employment history—employers are not terribly fond of job-hoppers.

If you're strapped for cash, it's better to take a job as a temporary worker or get a part-time position to pay the bills rather than to accept a job that doesn't fit. Then you can take the time necessary to find a position that meets all of your personal and professional needs. In the long run, you'll be much happier and much more successful.

Chapter 14

Special interview situations

If you've read Chapters 1 through 13 and you've done the recommended research, you're now well-prepared to handle most interview situations. But there are some scenarios in which you must adjust your presentation strategy slightly or use skills not called for in standard interviews. A telephone interview, for example, requires some different communication techniques than a face-to-face interview, and an out-of-town interview involves some considerations that don't come up when your interview is close to home. Similarly, certain types of interviewers demand "special handling." You may encounter unfriendly interviewers, interviewers who are extremely nervous or interviewers who are more interested in your potential as a romantic partner than your professional abilities. This chapter explores these and other special interview situations and shows you how to maneuver your way through them successfully.

"We'd like you to take a little test..."

Some employers require that would-be employees pass a variety of tests as part of the hiring process. You may be asked to take a drug test, psychological test or skills test on the day of your interview or before your final hire is approved.

If the employer requires you to take a drug test, you should be aware that some prescription drugs and foods, such as poppy seeds, can cause blips on a drug-testing radar screen. Talk to a doctor if you're concerned that any medications you take or foods you eat may cause false positives in a drug test.

Psychological tests typically are designed to get a fix on whether you're an ethical person and whether your personality is suited to the corporate culture. There's really nothing you can do to prepare for these tests, and you shouldn't try to outsmart the examiner by checking the answers you think the company wants to hear. The experts who review your answers can tell if you're trying to pretend you're someone you're not, and that will count against you far more than if you give the "wrong" answers. Answer the questions honestly—using some discretion, of course. I don't think I'd admit that I once had homicidal feelings toward my last boss or that I thought it was okay to take home pens and paper clips from the office.

If you're asked to interview with a corporate psychologist, just relax and be yourself. You are what you are, and if the psychologist doesn't think that your personality matches the job, well, maybe it's true. Think of psychological tests and interviews as additional tools to help you determine whether this is the right employer and job for you.

Skills tests, however, are a different matter. You can and should prepare for these tests. Before your interview, review the list of major skills you ranked as most important to the employer in Chapter 11. Then think about how the employer might ask you to demonstrate those skills and how you will respond. If you need to brush up on a particular skill, do so.

"Just fill out this application, please"

Even if the employer has a copy of your resume, you may have to fill out an employment application as a formality. Fill in all blanks completely, marking "Not Applicable" or "NA" in any spaces that don't apply to you. If you leave a line blank, the employer may suspect that you're not being totally forthcoming.

There is one exception to this rule, however. If the application asks you to state your salary requirements, don't provide a specific figure or range. Simply write, "Negotiable" or "Open." You don't want to tip your hand on salary at this point, for reasons we'll discuss later.

If you're asked to indicate your current or last salary, use as much latitude as possible, because employers often base their salary offers on your answer. Note that when I say, "use latitude," I don't mean that you should lie; I mean that you should include the value of all benefits, perks and bonuses in the figure you state. If your salary last year was $20,000 but you earned $5,000 in benefits, vacation pay and bonuses, write down "$25,000 salary package." In other words, specify the total value of your compensation, not just your base salary.

When you're filling out the job application, don't dawdle, because employers sometimes make note of how long it takes you to complete the form. If you need 30 minutes to fill out an application that other people finish in 10, the employer may assume that you're not exactly on top of things. Have your resume close at hand so you can complete the application as quickly and thoroughly as possible. And print legibly! Poor handwriting is a strike against you. (A good tip: Use a pen with erasable ink.)

Campus recruiting interviews

Many companies send interviewers to college campuses to recruit soon-to-be graduates. Typically, this is a grueling experience for both interviewer and interviewee. The interviewer must endure about 10 hours of back-to-back interviews. The interviewee, on the other hand, has the unenviable task of trying to stand out from the masses—not an easy job when you're one of 20 or more people the interviewer meets in a day.

To win the campus recruiting marathon, it helps to understand the interviewer's frame of mind, says Clay Barnard, director of career planning and placement at Case Western Reserve University. "In most cases," he explains, "campus recruiters are sent to bring back the blue-chip students. They are really under the gun because they know they'll be evaluated on the basis of the people they bring back to the company. If you keep that in mind, you understand how focused you need to be as a candidate. The more you know the industry and the better you can tie your skills and competencies to the employer's problem areas, the more likely it is that you'll be invited to a second interview. You must be very well-prepared because usually you only get a half-hour to make your case."

You learned in earlier chapters that it's important to describe your accomplishments and experiences in a way that helps the interviewer remember you. In campus recruiting sessions, that's doubly important. For example, if you worked as an intern at some business, don't just tell the interviewer that you obtained on-the-job experience during an internship with such-and-such corporation. Instead, describe in colorful detail a particular problem you solved or challenge you overcame during your internship.

Displaying enthusiasm is also especially critical in these interviews. That's easy enough when you only have one interview scheduled, but during the typical campus recruiting season, you may have two, three or even more interviews in one day. Often, several interviewers you want to meet all come to campus at the same time. Try to take at least a 10-minute break between interviews to realx and refocus your energy. It's tough to show the same enthusiasm to the last interviewer of the day as you do for the first, but if you want to maximize your job opportunities, that's what you have to do.

Out-of-town interviews

When you travel to a distant location to explore a job opportunity, you must deal with a special bit of interview etiquette: the issue of travel, hotel and dining expenses. If the company is picking up the tab, be very selective about what expenses you turn in for reimbursement. Although employers won't expect you to stay in some dumpy $21-a-night motel or eat every meal at McDonald's, neither will they look kindly on your hitting them up for a night at the ritziest joints in town. Employers regard the way you handle travel expenses as an indication of how you'll handle expenses on the job; if you're loose with their money now, they figure, you'll be just as hazardous to their budget if you're hired.

To be on the safe side, ask the person who arranges the interview for hotel and restaurant recommendations. And don't nickel-and-dime the employer to death, turning in receipts for every candy bar or newspaper you buy on your trip. Stick to the major expenses: hotel, cab fare, air fare and meals.

Another good strategy for out-of-town interviews is to arrive the day before your interview. That way, you can get a good night's sleep and arrive at the interview fresh and rested instead of frazzled and worn out from the trip.

All-day interviews

Most interviews don't last more than 30 or 60 minutes. But sometimes, the employer may want you to spend several hours or even an entire day meeting with different company personnel. You may be interviewed by the head of personnel at 8 in the morning, meet with a first-line supervisor at 9:30, talk to the department manager at 11, go to lunch with the staff at noon and meet half a dozen other people in the afternoon. And it's entirely possible that all of those different people will ask you exactly the same questions.

This can be very tiring, but try not to let your fatigue show. When you hear "Tell me about your accomplishments" for the tenth time, remember that this is all new to the interviewer. Answer with the same enthusiasm and interest as you did the very first time you were asked the question. Be consistent in your answers, too. You can bet that everyone will get together after the interview to compare notes.

It's a good idea to tuck a candy bar or other snack into your briefcase before your interview. If you feel your energy waning during the day, ask to take a 10-minute break. Duck into the restroom, eat your snack and freshen up a bit. Then go back out and greet the next interviewer with the same big smile you had when you arrived that morning.

The restaurant interview

Interviews that take place over a meal involve an extra stress component. In addition to worrying about what you're going to say to the interviewers, you have to worry about spilling your soup in your lap. Then there are all those rules of dining etiquette to remember, such as who picks up the check and which fork is used for what course—it's as bad as going out to dinner on a first date.

If you're unsure that your table manners are up to par, ask a friend who is in the know to critique you on a practice lunch or dinner before your interview. You should be able to pick up the basics of forks, knives and so on without too much trouble.

Aside from that, the most obvious tip is to order something that's easy to eat. Get the salad instead of the barbecued ribs or the fried chicken, for example. Never drink alcohol, even if the interviewers do. You want to keep every wit you've got about you. And just as you shouldn't smoke in an interviewer's office, you shouldn't light up in a restaurant, even if you're sitting in the smoking section.

As far as the check is concerned, leave it for the interviewers; they expect to pay. Don't use that as an excuse to go hog-wild and order every fancy dish you ever wanted to try, however. Order from the middle-price range of the menu.

If the employer invites you to bring your spouse to the luncheon or dinner, consider a few factors before you accept or decline the extra invitation. Is your spouse supportive of you and your career? Will your spouse's professional demeanor enhance or detract from your image? I know that sounds harsh, but the truth is that you will be judged not just on your own merit, but on your spouse's as well. If there's a chance that your spouse might slide in a few digs at your expense or otherwise reflect badly on you, simply tell the interviewer that your better half has other commitments. (What you tell your spouse is up to you.)

If you happen to be married to an old-fashioned husband, you should be especially wary of having him join you. Even if he's an absolute dear, he may unintentionally make comments that cast you in the role of the "little woman" or the "ultimate mother," which is just the opposite of the image you want to create.

If you do bring your spouse along, lay down a few ground rules before your interview. Agree that this is your day in the sun and that you'll be the one doing most of the talking. If the interviewer is a man, he and your husband may otherwise fall naturally into some conversation that leaves you out in the cold. As with standard interviews, do your best to keep the conversation focused on the job and your qualifications.

Committee interviews

You may encounter the particularly stressful scenario known as the committee interview, in which a whole group of people interview you at the same time. Some employers use this approach to see how you perform under stress; others use it simply in the interest of saving time.

Whatever the employer's motivation, the techniques for succeeding in a committee interview are the same. First, heighten your listening skills. Each person on the committee may have different priorities and a different communication and personality style. You must listen and observe everyone closely so that you can address each person's concerns and create rapport with the entire committee. Try to maintain good eye contact with everyone in the group and to address people by name when you answer their questions.

In addition, don't be afraid to pause and reflect before you answer a question. That's really hard to do when a roomful of people are staring at you, but a brief period of silence not only helps you come up with a more coherent answer, it helps you retain some control of the interview.

The stress interview

Some interviewers, evidently assuming that the standard interview situation isn't already difficult enough, use tactics to induce unnatural stress into the meeting. For instance, they may respond to one of your questions or statements with a prolonged silence, or they may make a highly controversial remark and then say, "Don't you agree?"

If this happens to you, remain calm, because that's exactly what the interviewer is trying to see if you can do. Understand that in most cases, the interviewer is simply playing a little testing game, and you just have to play along. Respond to an overly long silence with a smile and expectant expression; don't rush in to fill the gap. If the interviewer makes some outrageously offensive comment, you can either ignore it or just say something to deflect it, such as: "I guess we'll have to agree to disagree on that point. But I do agree with you on this issue of budget control, and..."

Telephone interviews

Many employers screen potential job candidates by phone before bringing them in for a face-to-face interview. These telephone screening interviews are tricky because you and the interviewer both must work without visual cues.

You can't read the interviewer's face and body language to assess how your comments are being received, so you must listen for changes in voice tone and inflection to get that information. In addition, because the interviewer can't see your smiling face or attentive body language, you must project your enthusiasm and interest with your voice. The secret to doing that is to smile as you speak. To remind yourself to smile, look in a mirror while you talk or, if that's too distracting, just put a big sign that says, "Smile!" near the phone. Remember that the telephone often distorts sound, so speak clearly and slowly.

If you know in advance when the interviewer will be calling, do your best to make sure that you won't be interrupted during the conversation. If you're taking the call at home, hire a sitter to take the kids to the park; if you have call-waiting, disable it if possible; and put the dog outside or in the basement. If the interviewer calls you unexpectedly at work and you can't speak freely, make an appointment to call back. Simply explain that you're very interested in discussing the subject but that it's impossible to do so presently because you are at work.

During the interview, remember that your goal is to convince the interviewer that you're worth bringing in for a face-to-face meeting. Usually, telephone screeners simply want to verify that you have the basic qualifications for the job. They probably won't want you to launch into a full-fledged presentation of your accomplishments and skills.

If you've already sent the company your resume, you may wonder why another rundown of your experience is requested by the company. There are two reasons. The first is to find out whether you can communicate in a professional, friendly manner. The second is to see whether you give the same accounting of your work history and experience as you provided on your resume. Although they probably won't tell you so, telephone screeners will have a copy of your resume in front of them when they call. You should have a copy on your desk as well, so that you're singing from the same song sheet. And even though you know well and good that telephone screeners already have all of your professional information, don't act annoyed or offended about having to provide it again. Be sure to jot down the skill areas and qualifications that the interviewer asks about; those are obviously the most important to the employer. You can refer back to these notes when planning your strategy for a face-to-face interview.

Telephone screeners also usually ask about your salary requirements. As in other types of interviews, it's best to counter with "I would entertain your best offer" or to state the going market range for the position. Otherwise, you may eliminate yourself from consideration.

Interviews with recruiters

You should approach interviews with search firms and placement firms as you would any other interview. Be just as professional, just as enthusiastic and just as sales-oriented as if you were interviewing with an employer. Don't think that because the person who interviews you at a search or placement firm isn't the "real" employer, you can relax.

Remember that executive-search firms—also known as retained search firms, headhunters and executive recruiters—are working for the employer, not the job-hunter. The same is true of some temporary-employment services and placement firms. Their main goal is not to find you a job, but to find the employer the right employee. They stake their professional reputation on the quality of the individuals they send to their clients, so you must convince them that you'll be a good reflection on their company if they recommend you to employers.

For the most part, you shouldn't say or do anything you wouldn't say or do in a regular job interview. Don't bad-mouth a former employer, spread industry gossip or behave unprofessionally. However, do be forthcoming about your salary requirements so you won't be sent on interviews for jobs that don't pay as much as you want.

If there's anything in your professional background that might cause an employer to react negatively to you, it's best to discuss it with the recruiter. Most search and placement firms conduct their own background checks on candidates, so the recruiter probably already knows about your situation anyway. If you do manage to keep some blemish on your record a secret from the recruiter, you run the risk that the employer will find out the truth in your interview or during a background check and hold the recruiter accountable. That only needs to happen once before the recruiter refuses to deal with you again.

However, this doesn't mean that you need to confess all of your sins in great detail; a short explanation will do. Remember that the recruiter is not a therapist or a dear old friend, but the person who decides whether to recommend you to an employer. Admit your mistakes, explain what you learned from them, and then move on to a new subject, just as you would in a job interview. In other words, accentuate the positive, downplay the negative.

The romantic interviewer

Several of my female friends have had the uncomfortable experience of being interviewed by men who were more interested in dating them than hiring them. In a couple of cases, after sitting through two or three interviews with the gentlemen in question, my friends determined that they weren't really being considered for any job. The whole "interview" was just a ruse the men were using to meet women.

If you suspect that you're being interviewed as a prospective dating partner and not an employee, ask for very specific information about the job and the timetable on the hiring decision. Try to talk to other employees as well—you'll probably be able to tell either by their comments or their expressions if the interviewer is a slimy operator.

If an interviewer makes unwanted advances toward you, try using responses such as the following to finesse your way past them:

> "I'm very flattered that you find me an interesting person. I'd like to tell you a little more about my professional background, because I think you'll find me to be very qualified for this job as well. For example..."

"Oh, you're very kind. By the way, would you tell me a bit more about..."

If you're really offended by the interviewer's behavior, you do, of course, have the option of reporting it to the interviewer's superior or even to the proper legal authorities. Sexual harassment is every bit as illegal as gender discrimination. As the Anita Hill debacle so painfully illustrated, however, you may have a tough time proving your case, and you probably will say good-bye to any chances you have of getting the job. Then again, you should ask yourself whether you really want to work for a company that fosters such behavior. You may decide that it's better to cut your losses and find a more businesslike employer.

The hostile interviewer

An acquaintance of mine once had an interview that began with the interviewer announcing: "I really don't know why I'm interviewing you. I don't think a woman is right for this position, and I want to make it clear up-front that we're only here today as a favor to the division head, who seems to like you."

I hope that you'll never have to deal with an interviewer who's that openly hostile, but I wouldn't be honest if I didn't warn you that you may, on occasion, find yourself talking to an interviewer who clearly has a negative attitude. Establishing rapport with such an individual is not easy, but it is possible.

The first thing to determine is whether the interviewer truly has hostile feelings toward you or is simply having a lousy day. It's very possible that the interviewer just had a fight with a spouse, was criticized by a boss or is completely stressed out. If that's the case, it's in your best interest to try to reschedule the interview. You can say something like, "I sense that this may be a really bad time for us to talk. If you want to reschedule, I'd be more than happy to do that." (Be sure to say this with a big, understanding smile. Act annoyed, and you'll exacerbate the situation.) If the interviewer doesn't want to reschedule, at least you've broken the ice a little. Your expression of sympathy may be all it takes to get the interviewer's mind and mood back on track.

What should you do if you determine that the interviewer's hostility is directed toward you? Stay cool, remember your chemistry-building skills and do your best to find some area of common ground. If you can hit on some subject that is near and dear to the interviewer's heart, you may be able to break down the walls between you.

If you can't diffuse the interviewer's hostility, often the most effective tactic is to make it clear that you're not intimidated. People who are openly aggressive usually seem to respect you more if you hold your ground than if you run away cowering. But there's an art to this—you have to put forth your own strength in a way that doesn't weaken the other person.

Let's say that you do come across a hostile and openly chauvinistic interviewer, for example. Don't go on the offensive, responding with a statement such as, "You're really in the dark ages about women, aren't you?" The worst thing you can do is get defensive or hostile in return; you'll only increase the person's anger level. Instead, validate the interviewer's concern and then offer evidence to overcome the objection:

> "I can see that you have some real concerns about the fact that I'm a woman. I can understand that, because a lot of employers think that women don't have the proper experience or attitude to deal with this sort of job. But I think if I tell you about some of what I've been able to accomplish, you'll see that you don't need to have those concerns about me."

Realize, however, that you're not likely to talk such interviewers out of their prejudices completely. The best you can hope for is to earn some level of professional respect—which, given the situation, would be a very positive outcome. You should also think carefully about joining any company that allows an interviewer who is openly hostile to women to continue to operate. It doesn't say much for the company's idea of "equal opportunity."

The non-interviewer

Nervous and inexperienced interviewers can be just as problematic as hostile or romantic interviewers. Because they're uncomfortable with the interview process, these interviewers often take the route of least resistance. That is, they don't really interview you at all. They tell you all about the position and the company, but they don't ask any questions about you. Or they get sidetracked on an issue that's more comfortable for them to discuss—a hobby, a favorite sports team, a day-care dilemma. This puts you in a bind. When interviewers don't ask any questions about you, they don't learn about all the wonderful things you have to offer.

If the interviewer doesn't take the initiative to ask you about your qualifications or to offer details about the job, you must find a way to work those topics into the conversation. Try using statements such as:

"Getting back to this job,..."

"If you don't mind, I'd like to share with you some of my experiences that are related to this job..."

"I have a few questions about..."

Be careful not to exert too much control over the interview, however. Make your moves subtly. Remember that interview etiquette says that you are the guest and the employer is the host, so you may offend the interviewer if you try to take over. If you want to steer the interviewer toward a particular topic, don't just say, "I really think we should talk about my accounting skills now." A better and more gracious alternative is to open with a question, such as:

"I'd like to hear more about the accounting aspect of this job. Could you tell me about the particular accounting issues that you'd like to resolve in your department?"

After the interviewer describes those issues, you can launch into your qualifications by saying something like,

"I've had some experience that will be valuable in trying to fix that problem. For example..."

Preparation is always the key

When you boil it all down, the basic strategies for navigating these sometimes difficult interview waters aren't that different from those you should use in standard interviews. In each scenario, you listen and observe closely, figure out what's going on in the interviewer's mind and then respond appropriately. You also prepare yourself for any eventuality so that you're not caught off-guard, left stammering and sputtering or looking like a deer caught in the headlights. As before, if you do your homework, you'll be able to impress any type of interviewer, in any interview situation.

Chapter 15

Rehearsal time!

By now, you've probably envisioned your upcoming interview a thousand times and practiced your sales pitch in your head just as often. You should congratulate yourself for having done so, because you're already much more prepared than most job applicants.

However, there's one more step you can take to make your interviewing skills even stronger: Stage a dress rehearsal.

Ask a friend to play the role of the employer, and conduct a mock interview. Give your friend the sample questions and answers you wrote down after reading Chapter 12 and the self-assessment sheets you created in Chapter 11. Then instruct your friend to ask you any 15 or 20 questions presented in Chapter 12. As you work your way through the interview, your friend should note how your answers compare with the answers you wrote down and whether you mention the important skills and accomplishments listed in your self-inventory.

Before you begin, create a setting that's as close as possible to the environment you expect to encounter in your actual interview. If your interview is to take place over a meal, for example, conduct the mock interview at your dinner table, complete with food, silverware and the works. Note, too, that this is a dress rehearsal, which means that you should put on your interview suit and fix your hair and makeup as you plan to do on interview day.

Do not refer to your answer sheets, skills inventory or company-research notes as you answer your "interviewer's" questions. You shouldn't take these notes into your real interview, either—you'll look pretty unsure of yourself if you need a cheat sheet to describe your abilities and accomplishments. You can, however, use notes to remind yourself of the questions you want to ask the interviewer. If you haven't already made up a list of such questions, do so before your mock interview. (Review Chapter 13 if you need help.)

Begin the mock interview as you will begin your real interview—by greeting the interviewer with a smile and a handshake. Then continue on clear through to your closing statement and parting handshake. Tell your friend not to interrupt the interview if you leave out some important fact or phrase something inappropriately. Instead, he or she should underline the relevant material on your answer sheets or skills inventory so you can discuss it after the interview concludes.

Lights, camera, action!

Now for the fun part. To get the most out of your dress rehearsal, make a video recording of it. Set up the video camera so that your entire body is in view, not just your head.

If you don't own the equipment you need, borrow or even rent it, because this exercise provides you with information you just can't get any other way. You can evaluate your body language, your facial expressions and your appearance from the interviewer's perspective. It's likely that you use some speech patterns or mannerisms that detract from your overall interview image, and it's much easier to detect these flaws when you can see and hear them on tape. You may even decide that you need to make adjustments to your outfit or to your makeup after watching your video.

It sounds silly, but...

I know you're probably thinking that this all sounds a bit goofy. And you and your friend will probably have a few giggles before the mock interview is over. That's okay—it will help reduce your anxiety a bit. But please don't ignore the importance of this exercise. It's the most powerful way to polish your interviewing skills and to evaluate your own performance. So give it a try, even if you feel a little foolish at first. You've got nothing to lose and much to gain.

Critique your performance

After the mock interview, review your videotape and critique your interview performance, using the following checklist as a guide.

Appearance

❏ Do I look like I'm dressed for business?

❏ Is my makeup subtle and conservative?

❏ Do I smile and look enthusiastic?

Body language

❏ Do I appear calm and confident, without displaying any nervous mannerisms?

❏ Is my posture attentive and interested?

❏ Is my handshake firm and confident? (Ask your friend for an evaluation.)

❏ Do I maintain an appropriate level of eye contact?

Presentation of skills

❏ Do I sound confident in my abilities?

❏ Is my language free of hedges, qualifiers or other expressions of uncertainty?

❏ Do I clarify vague questions?

❏ Do I attribute my success to my own ability instead of to luck or other outside factors?

❏ Do I acknowledge my successes instead of downplaying them?

❏ Do I back up my claims with accomplishments?

❑ Do I explain how my accomplishments affected the bottom line?

❑ Do I explain how the employer will benefit from my experience?

❑ Do I explain why I handled past projects and problems in a certain way?

❑ Do I emphasize the skills that are most important to the employer?

❑ Do I focus on the employer's needs instead of my own?

❑ Do I ask questions about the position and corporate culture?

❑ Do I maintain a 50/50 balance between talking and listening?

❑ Do I ask the appropriate closing questions?

You probably will need to watch your video several times to evaluate all of these factors. During one viewing of your tape, turn off the sound on your TV and watch the interview in fast-forward mode. This will exaggerate any nervous mannerisms you use and make them easier to spot.

In addition to watching the video, review the notes your friend made during the interview. What skills did you forget to mention? What accomplishments did you skip? How could you have presented your qualifications more powerfully?

After you complete your evaluation, repeat the mock interview, this time focusing on correcting the errors you made in the first session. Continue evaluating your performance and repeating the interview until you can answer "yes" to all questions in the checklist and you're confident that your presentation is the best it can be.

Last-minute instructions

Along with conducting a dress rehearsal, you need to take care of a few other last-minute details. Attend to these a few days before your interview so you won't be rushing around like a mad-woman on interview day.

First, gather together the following items, which you should take to your interview: three or four copies of your resume; the list of questions you want to ask the interviewer; a notepad; and a pen and a pencil. Tuck your resume, notepad and list of questions in a professional-looking executive notebook (you can pick them up at office supply stores for around $10).

Second, be sure that you have clear directions to the interview site. Just in case you should have trouble en route to your interview, write down the phone number of the interviewer in your notebook.

Finally, relax! The night before your interview, review your notes one more time and then get a good night's sleep. If a bad case of nerves keeps you awake, don't drink alcohol as a remedy; it will interfere with your sleep instead of enhancing it. Don't take sleeping pills, either, or you'll awake groggy and tired. Instead, listen to a relaxation tape, drink a glass of warm milk or try these other relaxation strategies:

- **Do some deep-breathing exercises.** Inhale slowly, counting to 10 as you draw in a deep, full breath. Hold your breath for three counts, then exhale slowly, again counting to 10. Repeat until you feel calmer.

- **Envision your success.** In your mind's eye, play out a scene in which you do and say all the right things in your interview. Visualize yourself greeting the interviewer, responding with charm and savvy to every interview question, and finally, getting a job offer. In other words, replace thoughts about what might go wrong on your interview with thoughts about what might go well.

- **Lock up your worries.** Tell yourself that because worrying about your interview won't accomplish anything, you're going to put away your anxieties for the night—and then visualize yourself doing so. First, picture your interview in your head. Then, visualize yourself placing the interview scene—and all of the worries that go with it—into a small safe and locking the door. (When I tell my friends about this technique, they laugh, but it works for me, and it just might do the trick for you, too.)

You're ready

If you're still feeling a bit nervous in the hours before your interview, repeat the relaxation exercises described above or take a brisk walk to work off your excess adrenaline. Then take a deep breath, put on your biggest smile and go sell yourself as the talented, sensational person you are. You've done a lot of hard work to prepare yourself for your interview, and you can feel confident that your efforts will enable you to make a very positive impression on your potential employer. Good luck!

Chapter 16

After the interview

Your interview's over. You thank the interviewer, shake hands good-bye and let out a big sigh of relief. Now what?

Well, here's my guess: About two minutes after you leave your interview, you'll launch into a no-holds-barred critique of your performance, replaying in your mind all of the things you think you did wrong. You should have said this. You shouldn't have said that. Your hair looked awful, you forgot to smile at the receptionist, you kicked the interviewer's desk when you sat down—and so on and so on and so on.

Even for supremely confident individuals, such I-blew-it, I-know-they-didn't-like-me reactions are natural. In fact, if you don't suffer from at least a minor case of Post-Interview Syndrome, you're the exception to the rule. But try not to waste too much energy chastising yourself for your perceived mistakes. For one thing, you probably are judging yourself much too harshly; it's doubtful that the interviewer paid much attention to your errors or even noticed them. For another, you need that energy to complete some very important post-interview tasks.

Take an objective look

As soon as possible after you leave your interview, take a few minutes to reflect upon what went well and what didn't, but do so from an objective viewpoint and with a positive mindset.

Instead of thinking, "Look at everything I did wrong," say to yourself, "Here's what I'll do better the next time."

Take out your interview notes, think back on the conversation you had with the interviewer, and write down important accomplishments you forgot to mention, skills you didn't highlight enough or any other errors you want to correct. Writing this information down on paper will help you commit it to memory, so you'll be less likely to make the same mistakes twice.

Also make a list of the major points the interviewer stressed during your discussion—the skills needed for the position, the problems facing the company, etc. If you get called back for a second interview, this list will help you prepare. You can make it a point to play up the skills on the list and to address the specific problems the interviewer mentioned.

Write a thank-you letter

Your second post-interview project is to send a thank-you note to each person who interviewed you. Do this within two days after your interview.

I know you probably don't want to hear that this is necessary—most people despise writing such letters. But sending a thank-you letter is a ritual of interview etiquette that you simply must observe. This rule applies for telephone interviews as well as for face-to-face meetings. If you don't send a thank-you letter, the employer may assume that either you're no longer interested in the job or that you're ignorant of this courtesy.

Curiously enough, employers don't seem to pay much attention to what you actually say in your letter. Most simply attach your letter to your personnel file and don't give it another thought. It's the fact that you made the effort to write that counts.

This doesn't mean that you can get away with a sloppily written thank-you letter, however. Employers do notice if your letter contains misspellings, typographical errors or other blemishes, and a letter containing such mistakes hurts more than it helps. You don't have to write an award-winning sales letter, but you do have to produce a concise, professional-looking document.

Let's get down to specifics. First, the technical stuff:

• Keep your letter short—no more than one page. Two or three brief paragraphs will do.
• Type your letter on a high-quality typewriter or create it on a computer and then print it on a laser printer or ink-jet printer. Avoid dot-matrix printers, which produce unprofessional-looking type that's often hard to read.
• Use standard business stationery (8½ x 11-inch paper), not note cards. Stick with white, gray or beige paper—no pinks or wild fluorescent colors. Remember that this letter demonstrates your ability to communicate in a businesslike manner.
• Use a formal business-letter format. (Refer to a secretarial textbook if you need help.)

Now, what should you say in your letter? Begin by thanking the interviewer for taking the time to meet you. Then express again your interest in the job and your enthusiasm about the company.

Next, add a few lines to emphasize that you're qualified for the job. If the interviewer stressed a particular point or concern, restate how your experience will enable you to address that particular issue. You also may want to mention some topic of conversation that will help the interviewer remember you. If the two of you laughed about something or shared a common professional interest, for example, work it into the letter. Close the letter by repeating your appreciation for the interviewer's time and your interest in the position. (See examples on the next two pages.)

That's all there is to it—nothing fancy, complicated or overly "sales-y." Just a simple expression of gratitude for the interviewer's time and a reminder of your interest in the position.

Be sure to proofread your letter several times before you mail it. Ask someone else to read it, too, because it's easy to miss typos even when you look closely. Also double-check to make sure that the interviewer's name and title and the name of the company are spelled right. If you address "Ms. Mona Meyers" as "Ms. Mona Myers," she won't bother to read the rest of your letter.

June Wheeler Phillips
154 Ohio Circle
Houston, TX 77082
(713) 555-9832

December 15, 1995

Ellen Wright
Operations Manager
Wright Baby Pictures, Inc.
Houston, TX 77082

Dear Ms. Wright:

Thank you for taking the time to meet with me
yesterday to discuss the position of photographer's
assistant. I enjoyed learning more about Wright Baby
Pictures and the commercial photography business.

I left our meeting very excited about joining your
firm. Although it's clear that being a photographer's
assistant is a challenging job, I believe that my
photography experience will enable me to be
successful, even on those days when, as you put it,
"all the kids are crying and the moms are mad."

Again, I appreciate your consideration. I look forward
to hearing from you and to the possibility of
becoming part of your organization.

Sincerely,

June Wheeler Phillips

June Wheeler Phillips

Helene P. Bryan
324 Ingle Plaza
Depew, NY 14043

December 15, 1995

Michael Howard, Marketing Manager
Sumpter Ski and Cycle
21 Eversman St.
Depew, NY 14043

Dear Mr. Howard:

It was a pleasure meeting you yesterday and learning more about Sumpter Ski and Cycle. I appreciate the time you spent discussing the sales representative position with me, especially in the middle of a very hectic sales season.

During our conversation, you stressed that you're very concerned about getting your new line of mountain bikes into resort outlets in the New England area. I'm confident that with my experience as a manufacturer's rep for Boehm and Schumann Ski Wear and my contacts in New England, I can get the line off to a sensational start.

Thank you once again for your time and consideration. I'm excited about the possibility of joining your team, and I look forward to hearing from you.

Sincerely,

Helene P. Bryan

Helene P. Bryan

Re-evaluate the company and the job

After you drop your thank-you letters in the mail, spend some time thinking about everything you learned about the job and the company during your interview. Does the job really sound right for you? Do you think you can succeed in it? Does the corporate culture suit your personality and your way of working? Do the people who work at the company seem like people you'd like to be around every day? Does the salary range being offered seem appropriate?

As you consider these issues, jot down any questions or concerns that come to mind. Then you'll be prepared if the employer calls to invite you to a second interview—or better yet, to offer you the job.

The waiting is the hardest part

Assuming that you asked the right kind of closing questions at the end of your interview, you should know when the employer plans to move ahead with the hiring process. If you don't hear anything by that time, it's not necessarily a sign that you're no longer in the running. It could be that the hiring manager was called out of town or is dealing with an unexpected crisis. It could be that the person who has to approve the hiring decision is sick. Or it could be that the company just operates at a snail's pace when it comes to hiring—many do. The point is, the delay could be caused by any number of factors unrelated to you.

If you haven't received any word by a week after the expected decision date, call the interviewer to request an update. Ask when the company will be making a decision and restate your interest in the job. If that decision date, too, goes by without any action on the employer's part, call back again. It's okay to keep calling every two weeks or so until you get an answer. If you're considering another offer at the time, you can say so; if you are the leading candidate for the job, it may prompt the employer to speed up the works. But don't badger the company or express any irritation over the delay.

It is possible that the employer has offered the job to someone else and is simply waiting until the deal is firm to notify other candidates. The employer may want to keep other candidates "in reserve" in case the first-choice candidate turns down the offer. But whatever the reason for the delay, you don't want to miss out on other opportunities while you're waiting. Reasonable employers will understand this and so won't mind if you ask whether you're one of the top candidates for the job. If they say that you're not, you can concentrate on other possibilities.

If you didn't get the job...

If you are turned down for a position, it's a good idea to contact the hiring manager and ask what specific skills or qualifications you were lacking that put you out of the running. If you ask politely and professionally, without a hint of anger in your voice, most people will be happy to advise you. Don't ever argue with the hiring manager on this point, however—you want to maintain a very friendly, enthusiastic image. It just may be that the person who got the job won't work out or that some other position for which you're better suited will open up, so don't burn your bridges. To reinforce the hiring manager's positive image of you, follow up your conversation with a thank-you letter that expresses your appreciation for the advice.

Make a vow, too, not to take the employer's decision as a personal rejection. It's not a reflection of your worth, nor is it a sign that no employer will want you. Somebody else simply had qualifications that met the employer's needs more closely. In fact, it may be that qualifications had nothing at all to do with the decision—it could be that the candidate who got the job did so because she was the hiring manager's cousin's girlfriend. Take another look at your skills inventory and your resume, and remind yourself of just how much you have to offer. Then get back on the job-hunting trail and use everything you learned while interviewing for this job to make your next interview even better.

Chapter 17

How to play the salary game

"We'd like to make you an offer." No sweeter words were ever spoken—at least, not to someone looking for a job.

I remember the first few times in my professional career that I heard those words. On the first occasion, I had just graduated from college and was trying to land a job in the crowded field of television production. The next two times, I was desperate to quit jobs I hated. In all three instances, I was so excited to get an offer that I accepted on the spot. No negotiation, no thinking it over, no asking for details. You want me, you got me.

I'll never know how much those hasty decisions cost me. I do know that in at least one case, I accepted a full 30 percent less in salary than co-workers with the same title and level of responsibility. If you added up all of the money I would have made if I had been a smarter negotiator—well, let's just say that it makes me a little sick to think about it.

If you want to avoid making similar mistakes, you must become a master at the art of salary negotiation. You must not only learn how the salary game is played in today's workplace, but you must understand the proper mental approach to take in the negotiation process.

In this chapter, we'll look at the basics of salary negotiation. Then, in Chapter 18, you'll learn the specific steps involved in negotiating for salary, benefits and other compensation.

How the game is played today

Perhaps the most perplexing aspect of negotiating a salary is that the rules of the game vary from company to company. Some employers refuse to negotiate at all. They offer one salary, and if you don't accept it, they simply offer the job to the next person. Obviously, employers can operate nicely under this policy when the marketplace is flooded with many similarly qualified candidates.

Other employers use a pay-grade system. They evaluate each job in the company and assign it a pay-grade level, such as Secretary I or Data Analyst II, and then they set a specific salary range for each grade. They may negotiate salaries to an extent, but only within the confines of the established salary range for the job. Typically, the first offer made to a candidate falls at the bottom or middle of the salary range. Employers don't like to hire people in at the upper end of the range because then they can't give annual raises without moving beyond the salary guidelines for the position.

Still other employers establish loose salary guidelines for a position, but aren't opposed to paying above—or below—the targeted salary when the situation warrants. If they want you very badly, they may be willing to raise the salary or add benefits to increase the value of the total compensation. Generally, smaller companies are more flexible in this regard.

The person handling the negotiation varies from company to company as well. In companies with HR departments, the HR representative often acts as a liaison between the candidate and the hiring manager. Other times, you deal directly with the hiring manager. Each situation has its pros and cons. HR personnel usually are more skilled at negotiation, which means they probably won't give you as many clues to what they're really thinking as the hiring manager. On the other hand, there are benefits to dealing with HR instead of the hiring manager. If negotiations get sticky when you're bargaining with the hiring manager, it could damage your working relationship after you're on the job.

Working with recruiting firms

If you landed the job through a search or placement firm, your recruiter may or may not be actively involved in the negotiation. If the recruiter is involved, don't assume that you can turn over the deal-making reins. Yes, it's usually in the recruiter's best interests to help you negotiate a good deal, especially when the agency's compensation depends upon your starting salary. But you're the one who ultimately has to live with the salary package, so you should be the one in charge. Do, however, ask the recruiter's advice. At the very least, the recruiter can provide insights on the employer's policy on salary negotiation and tell you whether the compensation being offered is appropriate.

Many recruiting firms work on a contingency basis—that is, they're paid only if the employer hires someone sent by the agency. Sometimes, unscrupulous employers try to cheat recruiters out of their fee by hiring on the sly. They offer you the job on the condition that you don't report it to the recruiter.

Be leery of such an offer. In the first place, the recruiter earned that fee fair and square, and you're just as guilty of unethical conduct as the employer if you take part in the scheme to cut the recruiter out of the deal. In the second place, an employer who thinks it's all right to be dishonest in this sort of business dealing will probably also think it's okay to treat you dishonestly when you're an employee.

The importance of your starting salary

Regardless of what salary policies the employer follows or who is involved in the negotiation, one important constant applies. After you take the job, it will be very difficult to increase your salary substantially, because employers base annual raises on your starting wage. In most companies today, the average annual raise is in the neighborhood of 3 to 5 percent. Some employers won't raise your salary much more than that even when they give you a promotion. If you work for such an employer, you'll be lucky if a promotion nets you an increase of 10 to 15 percent.

You can see, then, how critical it is to negotiate your best deal when you accept a new job. Your success or failure affects you for a long time to come.

How high can you go?

Your negotiating power depends on a variety of factors. The first is your negotiating skill—your ability to convince the employer to give you what you want. The second is the job market. If a lot of people are out there selling the same skills and experience as you, you lose some negotiating edge. As you well know, many people are looking for work right now, which means that in most fields, it's a buyer's market. Employers aren't as likely to negotiate salaries as in years past because they figure that if you turn down the job, they won't have that much trouble finding someone else with similar qualifications.

However, keep in mind that the employer selected you as the best of all the available candidates. You must have something the others didn't offer, so don't assume that a tight economy means you can't negotiate for a better deal. If you ask for additional compensation in the right way and your request is reasonable considering the market value of the position, you won't risk losing the job. You can always bring your asking price down if the employer says no—and the employer just may surprise you and agree to your request.

The third factor affecting your negotiating power is the type of job you're being hired to do. Generally, the higher up the corporate ladder you go, the more you can bargain for wages, benefits and perks.

A look inside the employer's head

When you negotiate salary, you must remember that you're involved in a sales process. Your goal is to persuade the customer—the employer—to pay top dollar for your services. Like other customers today, employers are extremely tight-fisted with their money. The only way to get them to part with more of it is to convince them that doing so will pay off handsomely for the company.

In Chapter 6, you learned that you must focus on the needs of the employer and not on your own needs when you sell yourself in an interview. The same applies in salary negotiations. Saying, "I need $5,000 more to meet my mortgage payments" won't get you anywhere. Employers don't care about your financial problems. They base their salary decisions on one thing only: how much value they think you'll add to the company. If you want $5,000 more than the employer offers, you have to prove you're worth $5,000 more to the company.

How do you do that? By reminding the employer of the benefits and advantages you offer and by citing examples of how your past accomplishments benefited previous employers. In other words, by using the same sales techniques you used to convince the employer to make you a job offer in the first place.

Negotiation strategies

The way in which you present your requests during salary negotiations has a dramatic impact on whether you get what you want from an employer. Be firm but flexible, self-confident but not arrogant or demanding, and sell your skills and knowledge in a way that appeals to the employer's concern about the bottom line.

1. Maintain the proper attitude

During negotiations, be enthusiastic, polite and professional. Don't approach the negotiation as a competition in which you and the employer are in opposing camps. Instead, let the employer know by your tone of voice and your demeanor that your goal is a win-win solution. If you are too pushy or adopt a "take-it-or-leave-it" attitude, the employer may get the impression that you're not that interested in the job and withdraw the offer.

2. Start high and work toward a middle ground

Ask for a little more than you think the employer wants to pay and then negotiate a middle ground between the employer's first offer and your counter-proposal. If the employer offers you $38,000 and you want $40,000, ask for $42,000 and then work backward toward your target salary.

3. Be creative

Look beyond base salary for ways to boost your income. For example, if the employer can't increase your base pay because of salary-grade restrictions, ask for a one-time sign-on bonus. Some other options to consider include:

- **Vacation days.** If new employees must work for a full year before receiving paid vacation days, ask that this restriction be waived. Or ask for a specified number of extra days off.
- **Early salary review.** If the employer normally reviews performance and salary only at one-year intervals, request that you be given a three-month or six-month review instead. Ask the employer to agree that if your performance is satisfactory, you'll receive your annual raise at that time instead of waiting a full year.
- **Bonuses.** In addition to requesting a sign-on bonus, you may be able to negotiate a performance bonus. Lay out a specific performance goal and suggest that the employer pay you a certain reward if you accomplish that goal.
- **Flextime or a shorter work week.** If time is more important to you than money, offer to accept the established salary in exchange for a flexible work schedule or for fewer hours. One woman I know, for example, accepted a lower salary with the understanding that she would work only 35 hours a week instead of the standard 40.

You also can negotiate for moving expenses and travel expenses, paid sick days or additional health, life, dental or disability insurance. If job titles are important to you, you can ask for a more impressive title. However, don't accept a title in lieu of fair monetary compensation—remember, you can't buy groceries with job titles.

4. Continue selling yourself

As you negotiate, remind the employer how the company will benefit from your service. Let's say, for example, that the employer balks at giving you $8,000 more in compensation. Explain how you will recoup that amount and more for the company. For instance:

> *"I realize that you have a budget to worry about. However, remember that with the desktop publishing skills I bring to the position, you won't have to hire outside vendors to produce your monthly customer newsletter and other publications. That alone should produce far more than $8,000 in savings a year."*

In other words, justify every additional dollar or benefit you request. Remember to do so by focusing on the employer's needs, not yours.

5. Ask a fair price

Don't ask for the moon; you won't get it. Be sure that your requests are reasonable and in line with the current marketplace. If the market rate for a position is $35,000 to $45,000, don't ask for $65,000 and expect the employer to take you seriously.

If the salary offer is below market value, gently suggest that it's in the company's best interests to pay the going rate:

> *"The research that I've done indicates that the going rate for a position such as this is $5,000 higher than this offer. Although I'd really like to work for you, I can't justify doing so for less than market value. I think if you reevaluate the position and consider its importance to your bottom line, you'll agree that it's worth paying market price to get someone who can really make an impact."*

6. Be a confident negotiator

Part of convincing employers that you're worth a certain amount is convincing them that you believe you're worth that much. If you appear nervous, squirming in your seat or wringing your hands while you talk salary, it's a dead giveaway to the employer that you're not sure you deserve the amount you requested. Remember to use the confident body language and speech patterns you learned about in earlier chapters.

Silence is another important weapon in creating this confident image. When you make a salary request, don't go on and on, stating over and over again why it's justified. Make your request and offer a short, simple explanation of why that amount is appropriate.

"I believe that given the market value of my experience and of this position, the compensation should be $5,000 higher."

After you state your request, be quiet. Don't rush in to fill any silence that ensues; wait for the employer to respond. If you don't, you appear uncertain in your request and let the employer know you're probably willing to settle for less.

7. Let the employer win, too

It's a smart negotiating strategy to ask for a few benefits or perks you don't want that badly. Then you can "give in" and agree to take the job without those added benefits if the employer meets all of your other requests. In other words, you let the employer win these points in the negotiation.

Ideally, both parties in a negotiation should come away from the table feeling that they've won. This is especially true when you're dealing with salary negotiations. You want employers to have good feelings about the price paid for your services so that your working relationship begins on a positive note.

Women as negotiators

Chapter 2 discussed the fact that women typically aren't very good at salary negotiation. Because we're raised in a culture that often undervalues women, we tend to underestimate our worth in the workplace, too. Consequently, we often settle for lower salaries than men.

Some experts suggest that women are afraid to ask for what they're worth because they fear rejection. If they ask for a certain amount and the employer says no, they feel hurt that the employer doesn't value them more. They don't want to experience that hurt, so they don't risk initiating it.

If you suffer from this fear, you're taking salary negotiation too personally. A salary is not an indication of your worth as a human being; it's a reflection of the market value of a certain set of skills and qualifications. This is a business deal, pure and simple. You know the fair market price for someone with your skills (at least, you should if you did the recommended research in Chapter 10). Don't hesitate to ask for that amount. You are not a human blue-light special.

Another reason that some women don't negotiate as hard as men, say researchers, is because they simply don't value money as much. They consider it less important than things like personal relationships and a sense of community. These priorities are very noble ones, and the world would be a much better place if everyone thought in the same terms. The problem is that when you accept a salary that's beneath market value or lower than what your peers earn for doing the same job, it's hard not to become resentful or angry. Those feelings detract from your job satisfaction and also hinder your success. However much you may dislike the negotiation process, however much you'd prefer to focus on other things, you cannot afford to take this aspect of your working life lightly.

Be willing to walk away

Obviously, the less you want the job, the easier it is to negotiate. You're not afraid to ask for more because you don't have as much invested emotionally in the outcome. If you go into negotiations with the attitude that you must have this particular job, on the other hand, you're in real trouble. The employer will notice your desperation and may offer you less than top price—and you'll take it, because you want the job so badly.

In the days or weeks before your salary negotiations, don't spend too much time envisioning yourself in the job. You'll build the position up in your mind to such an extent that you may be willing to settle for any salary just to get the job. Instead, when you think about the job, also think about alternative options you can pursue if this one doesn't work out. Entering your negotiations in this frame of mind puts you in a much stronger, much more confident position and vastly improves your chances of striking a good salary deal.

Chapter 18

The negotiation process

In salary negotiation, as in any negotiation, you must work carefully and thoughtfully to achieve your goals. It's a delicate situation, and a misstep can cost you money—and possibly, the job. Now that you understand the underlying psychology involved in salary negotiation, let's take a closer look at the specific moves and counter-moves you need to make at each point in the process.

Arm yourself with information

The salary negotiation process is a bit like a poker game in which each player tries to get the other one to lay down cards first. Employers want to know how much money you want before they tell you what salary they have in mind. If your figure is lower than their figure, they can revise their offer downward and save some money. You, on the other hand, want the employer to come clean first. That way, you don't ask for less than the employer is willing to pay.

There are two keys to coming out ahead in this buyer-seller game. The first is information. You need to know what salaries other employers in your area pay for similar jobs and how much someone with your level of experience usually earns. (Chapter 10 explains in detail how to find this information.) You also should try to learn something about the employer's pay policies—whether the company uses a salary-grade structure, whether it has a firm rule about not negotiating salaries, whether it's known for paying higher or lower salaries than its competitors, and so forth. All of this information is critical to determining whether you're being offered a fair wage and also to negotiating a good deal.

Timing is everything

The second secret to successful salary negotiation is timing. To gain the most bargaining power, wait until after the employer offers you the job to name a specific price for your services. At that point, you have some negotiating advantage, because you know that the employer thinks that you, more than any other candidate, offer the solution to the company's problems.

If you state a specific salary before the employer arrives at that decision, you not only lose negotiating power, you run the risk of eliminating yourself from the competition. Name a figure that's above the established salary range, and the employer may assume that the company can't afford you. Name a figure that's too far below the established range, and the employer may think you're willing to work for less because you don't have the appropriate skills or because of some other character flaw.

However—and this is an important however—you should discuss a salary range with the employer during the interviewing process. You need to determine whether buyer and seller are in the same ballpark. If you're not, you may want to reconsider pursuing the job further. If you are still interested in the job, you can start thinking about how you might convince the employer to raise the salary range for the position.

Again, it's to your advantage to get the employer to name a range first. When interviewers ask you about your salary expectations, try to hit the ball back into their court with a statement such as:

"I need to know more about the job before making a firm salary decision, but I will certainly entertain your best offer. What range did you have in mind?"

You may want to press a little further and ask, "Where would someone with my qualifications fit into that range?" This information will help you decide what salary to request when actual negotiations begin.

If the interviewer won't name a range and insists on knowing yours, don't be stubborn. It's in the best interests of both parties to get the issue on the table, so name whatever salary range you determined was appropriate during your research. Stating a salary range instead of a specific figure helps eliminate the chance that you'll overshoot the employer's target salary or fall way below it.

Always give a fairly broad range and reiterate your willingness to consider any offer:

"As I said, I'm open to considering any offer you might make. I'm sure that a company such as yours would pay a fair wage. According to my research, the going rate for this job, in this marketplace, is $40,000 to $52,000."

It's important that you understand how the employer processes this information, because where you think you fall in the range and where the employer thinks you fall are probably two different figures. When you name a salary range, you're usually thinking about the top of that range as your salary goal, but the employer usually hears the bottom end of the range. For that reason, the bottom of the salary range you specify should be the absolute minimum you will accept for the job. Don't name a salary figure that you aren't willing to take. You may even want to name a bottom salary figure that's a little higher than the actual market value, just to give yourself some negotiating room.

Be prepared at all times

At the end of each interview, analyze what you've learned about the position and reassess your asking price. You may determine that the salary range you established for the position is too high or too low. Perhaps, for example, you learned during your interviews that the job actually involves more responsibility than the job title reflects. The company assigned the label of "manager" to the position, but in real terms, the job is a director-level position. Or perhaps it's just the other way around. They call the job "director of customer service," but the truth is that you'd be a first-line manager over only five people. (Smaller companies, especially, tend to inflate job titles.) If the job sounds markedly different from the one on which you based your initial salary figure, do some additional research and calculation. You should be prepared with a firm salary range at all times so you can respond appropriately if the employer calls to offer you the job.

How to respond to a job offer

After the company makes you an offer, the real negotiating begins. Here are the steps you need to take to make the negotiation a successful one.

1. Express your enthusiasm

When you hear that magic phrase, "We'd like you to work for us," the first words out of your mouth should express your excitement about the offer. Enthusiasm is catching, and you want the employer to remain enthusiastic about you during the negotiation process. Telling the employer how pleased you are about the opportunity also sets a positive climate for the negotiation.

2. Ask for time to think it over

Never accept a job offer on the spot. You'll be too focused on the excitement of getting the offer to make a clear-headed decision. Take at least 24 hours to consider the offer—more, if possible.

If the salary is substantially lower than you can accept, give some indication of that when the offer is made. A good way to do this is to say something like the following:

"I've been very impressed with your company and I'd really like to work with you. I'm going to consider your offer very carefully, but I do want to let you know that the salary is a bit below what I had in mind. As I think about this, it would make me feel more comfortable if I knew there might be some flexibility in the compensation package."

By making this statement right away, you let the employer know that some salary negotiation is necessary. The hiring manager or the HR person handling the negotiation can then begin getting any necessary approvals to raise the salary level or look for other ways to sweeten the pot, such as offering a sign-on bonus or additional benefits. If the employer tells you that no flexibility is possible, you know before you consider the offer that the salary package isn't likely to be improved. It's always possible that the employer is bluffing at this point, of course, or that you'll be able to convince the employer to become flexible later on in the negotiation. But at the very least, you're forewarned that getting an increase in the offer will be difficult.

If the salary you're offered is higher than you expected, don't let on and don't rush to accept the job. This situation also calls for some careful consideration. It could be that you've underestimated your value on the market or that there's something about the position you neglected to take into account when you came up with your salary range.

3. Ask for details

If the employer does not provide them, ask for details about non-wage compensation—insurance benefits, paid vacation days and other perks that add value to the offer. You can say:

"As I'm considering your offer, it will help me to know about any benefits that I would receive in addition to salary. Can we please go over those now?"

Alternatively, you can ask for the name of the appropriate person in HR who can discuss these issues with you. Among the basic benefits you should inquire about are:

- **Health, dental, life and disability insurance.** Ask for specifics about coverage, especially for health insurance. Deductibles, benefit limits and other features vary widely from employer to employer and can make a significant impact on the total value of the compensation package. With the high cost of health care, it's not unreasonable to ask to see a copy of the company health plan.
- **Retirement or pension plans.** Find out whether the employer matches employee contributions to such plans and how long it takes to become vested in the plan (the number of years you must work at the company before you are entitled to your funds).
- **Overtime policies.** Will you be paid on an hourly basis, offered extra days off as compensation or be expected to work overtime with no additional pay? Do these policies apply to days you spend traveling on company business?
- **Profit-sharing plans.**
- **Vacation days and sick days.**
- **Tuition reimbursement** for training related to your job.
- **Employee discounts** on company products.

Depending upon the position, you may also want to inquire about the following:

- **A company car** or a car maintenance and gas allowance (for jobs involving automobile travel).
- **A termination contract** that specifies a certain severance payment if you're laid off before a set period of time (usually reserved for executive positions).
- **Stock options** (if the company is a publicly traded firm).
- **Moving expenses** (if the job requires relocation).

Also ask how and when the company awards raises to employees. Find out what you can reasonably expect in terms of annual increases and whether those increases are based on performance or simply on cost-of-living factors. If the company does reward employees based on performance, ask how your performance will be evaluated.

4. Evaluate the offer

When you assess the employer's offer, it's important to look at the big picture. Don't think just about base salary, but about the value of the total compensation package. Consider, too, whether the compensation will be acceptable to you in the future as well as today, given what you learned about the employer's pattern of wage increases.

Don't forget to factor in any expenses associated with the job. For example:

- How much money will you spend commuting to the job?
- If you have young children, how much will you spend on day care while you're at work?
- If you're moving to take a job, is the cost of living in the new location higher or lower than where you live now?

In addition to analyzing the offer in monetary terms, evaluate how much personal and professional satisfaction you will get from the job:

- Does this job fit in with your long-term career plans?
- Do you have a reasonable chance of being successful?
- How many hours will you be spending on the job?
- What, if anything, are you giving up if you take the job?
- Will you enjoy the corporate culture and is it one that values individuals like you?

One word of caution: Some employers, in an effort to convince you to take the job, promise future rewards. They may tell you, for example, that they plan to expand in the next four years and imply that if you come on board now, you'll be the first to head up a new division when the expansion occurs. Take all of this into consideration, but don't agree to work for less than fair-market value today in exchange for future benefits unless you're absolutely certain that you'll be paid back in full for your efforts. There's no guarantee that the employer will be willing or able to keep promises made to you.

If, after careful assessment of these issues, you decide you do want the job and the compensation seems appropriate, you may choose to accept the offer as is. If the offer is lower than you'd like and/or you think the employer may be willing to bump up the compensation a bit, it's time to plot your negotiating strategy.

5. Determine your bottom line

First, determine your bottom line—the minimum package of salary and benefits you will accept in exchange for your services. Next, create a "wish list" of the salary, benefits or perks you'd like to get over and above your bottom line. This is the compensation package you'll request at the beginning of your negotiation.

How much should you ask for? A little more than you think you can get. Shoot above the employer's target salary with the goal of working toward a middle ground that satisfies you both. Include on your wish list some benefits you're willing to concede, so the employer "wins" on those points.

However, as discussed in the last chapter, you should be sure that your requests are reasonable, considering the market value of the position and your experience. If your requests are too much above the norm, you'll look foolish, uninformed or, at the least, not serious about taking the job.

6. Accept, decline or start negotiating

At the appointed time, call the employer to give your answer to the offer. If you decided to take the offer as is, simply say you're accepting the position and you're thrilled about the opportunity. If you decided that you don't want the job no matter what the salary, turn down the position politely and professionally. Don't forget that although this particular job might not be right for you, you may want to be considered for future openings, so be very gracious in your rejection of the offer.

If you want to negotiate for a better deal, kick off the negotiating process with a statement such as:

"I've thought carefully about your offer, and I want to repeat that I'm very interested in joining the company. However, I do have some concerns about the compensation package that I'd like to discuss with you."

Then, using the negotiation strategies laid out in the preceding chapter and in the next section, work your way through your wish list until you're satisfied with the deal.

How to get past common salary objections

When you ask for more than was initially offered, it's likely that you'll encounter some resistance. Most employers will try to convince you to bring your price down, just as you'll try to convince them to raise their offer.

Employers typically cite a few standard reasons for not wanting to increase the compensation package. These include:

- "That's more than we allocated for the job."
- "You'd be earning more than others at that level."
- "That's all our budget will allow."
- "That's too much more than your last salary."
- "You've been out of the work force a while."
- "I'm sorry, but it's our policy not to negotiate."

Let's look at each of these objections and some strategies you can use to overcome them.

1. "That's more than we allocated for the job."

Your first strategy in this situation, obviously, is to convince the employer to revise the budget allocation for the position. To do that, you'll have to provide solid reasons why the allocation is not on target—in other words, demonstrate that the salary is below market value. As you learned in the last chapter, it's important to make your case politely and without a trace of resentment or annoyance. Emphasize your interest in the job again and then address the issue of fair market value:

"This position does sound perfect to me, but the salary level the company has established is below what other employers in the area are paying. Although I would really like to work for you, I can't justify doing so for less than market rate, which is $21,000 to $27,000."

2. "You'd be earning more than others at that level."

When you hear this objection, you can try one of two responses. The first is to persuade the employer that you should earn more because you're worth more. If you know, for example, that you have a more advanced college degree or more experience than others in the department, you can point that out as evidence of the additional value you'll bring to the company.

The second option is to suggest that you be given a different job title so that you fall in a higher salary range. You can suggest that you assume a few additional responsibilities to compensate for the higher salary. Understand, though, that this won't be an easy battle to win, especially in a large, very structured company. Employers don't like to fool with job titles and salary levels once they're assigned. Generally, you'll have a better shot at getting a job title changed if the company is small and doesn't use a formal pay-grade structure.

3. "That's all our budget will allow."

The company may very well be unable to provide you with a higher salary. If you think that the employer is being sincere about budget constraints, negotiate for non-cash benefits. For example, suggest that you'll accept the lower salary in exchange for a few hours off each week or for additional vacation days.

You should try to get some indication of when the employer expects the budget to improve. If there's not enough money to pay you market value now, there might not be enough next year, either. But if the employer expects a major turnaround soon—and you can find good evidence to support these expectations—you may want to negotiate for future compensation. Suggest that the two of you set specific performance goals for your first six months or year on the job and that you be awarded a certain bonus or salary increase if you meet those goals.

4. "That's too much more than your last salary."

Some employers try to base salary offers on how much you made in your last job. You must help the employer realize that your current or past salaries are irrelevant because the value of your last job has nothing to do with the value of the new job. You can say something like:

> *"You're right—I did earn substantially less on my last job. However, keep in mind that I've been in that job for three years, and the experience I've gained over that time certainly warrants an increase."*

Here's another alternative:

> *"I am paid much less at my current job than you're offering. However, as you're probably aware, I am underpaid in that position; the employer isn't paying market rate. Because that's one of the reasons why I'm considering leaving my current job, I wouldn't want to accept anything less than market value for a new job."*

5. "You've been out of the work force for a while."

If you're trying to break back into the working world after several years of unemployment, you may find that some employers expect you to work for less because of your absence. The logic, presumably, is that you won't be as productive as other employees because you'll need some retraining. Employers may also assume that you are desperate for a job because you haven't worked for a while.

You must prove that you offer the same skills as others with your same level of experience and therefore are worth full market value. You might ask the employer what skills you would need to earn market rate. Then you can remind the employer that you do offer those skills by pointing to your volunteer activities or other experience.

If that doesn't work, you can say that you'll take the lower salary with the understanding that your performance will be reviewed in three months. Ask the employer to agree that if you meet specific performance criteria—thereby proving that you're equally adept as everyone else with the same job title—your salary will be increased to the going market rate.

6. "I'm sorry, but it's our policy not to negotiate."

This is a tough one, because you must determine whether the employer is really being truthful. If you know from your networking contacts or other research that the employer's policy prevents salary negotiation, you probably shouldn't push your luck. But if you think that the employer may be willing to give a little, you can say:

> "I understand that you don't normally negotiate on the issue of salary. But I think that you may agree that an exception is warranted in this case because..."

Explain why the salary is not appropriate for the position and restate your salary request. Again, if the employer can't negotiate base salary, ask for noncash benefits to build the compensation package to an acceptable level.

Know when to quit

At some point in your negotiation, the employer will say that the company has reached its maximum offer. If you think that the employer may be bluffing, test your theory by saying politely:

> "I'd like to think over this offer tonight and give you an answer tomorrow. However, I think it's only fair to let you know up front that some compensation issues are still a concern to me. Before I make my decision, is there anything else we can do to resolve these issues?"

If the answer is no, accept the fact that the employer is either unable or unwilling to raise the compensation package further. Keep pushing beyond this point, and you'll annoy and anger the employer, possibly to the extent that the offer is withdrawn.

Should you accept a low offer?

Only you can answer that question. You must determine whether other aspects of the position, such as advancement potential, working conditions or job satisfaction, outweigh a salary offer that's less than it should be. If you do decide to accept the position, however, be sure that you can go into the job with a good attitude. If you feel any resentment about having to work for less than you wanted, you should probably decline the offer. A salary issue that bothers you now will frustrate you even more after you're on the job.

Solidify the deal

When you and the employer come to an agreement over salary and benefits, write a brief letter outlining the terms of the deal. Verbal agreements have a way of being ignored or forgotten after the negotiation is through. When you have a written document that details your agreement, on the other hand, it's more difficult for the employer to fudge on the terms later on.

Some employers make it a policy to send letters of agreement to all new hires, but in most cases, putting the deal in writing will be up to you. It's better to take on this task yourself than to ask the hiring manager or HR staff member to do it for you—they likely won't appreciate having to do more work on your behalf.

Unless you're taking an executive-level position, in which case you might want to consider having a lawyer draft a formal employment contract, this letter of agreement needn't be long or complicated. Begin the letter by restating your excitement about the offer, and then say something like, "To make sure that I haven't misunderstood any terms of our agreement, I've outlined the major points below." Then briefly list the base salary, benefits and perks the employer agreed to give you. Include any agreements about your job title, starting date and special performance bonuses (state the specific goals you're expected to meet along with the rewards you'll earn if you achieve those goals). Also note briefly your understanding of how and when your salary and performance will be reviewed.

Next, say that if you don't hear from the employer, you'll assume that your letter represents the agreement properly. (This relieves the employer of the chore of sending a formal response if everything is in order.) End the letter by emphasizing again that you're looking forward to being part of the company.

Saying good-bye to your old employer

Once you have a firm deal with a new employer, it's time to give your current employer the bad news. It's standard practice to give at least two weeks' notice when resigning.

Some companies now require that employees who leave the company go through an exit interview. The purpose of this interview is to give the employer an opportunity to learn about problems that cause employees to leave. If you're really unhappy at your current job, you'll probably be tempted to tell the employer exactly what you think about the company. Don't. No matter how difficult, swallow the urge to yell, "I'm leaving because you're all a bunch of creeps and this place is a nuthouse!" Never, ever burn your bridges behind you. You may need that bunch of creeps to provide you with a good reference some day—or you may change your mind and want to return to the nuthouse in a few years.

Be candid in your exit interview, but also be diplomatic. Explain why you're leaving without placing blame or getting into name-calling. You might even want to say, "If these problems are resolved down the road, I may be interested in coming back."

What if they make you a counteroffer?

When you turn in your resignation, there's always a chance that your current employer will match or raise the offer made by the new employer. You may be tempted to rush back to the new employer and use the counteroffer as leverage to get more money for the new job. Indeed, many people successfully play employers off against each other in this way. But before you try it, you should consider several issues carefully, because counteroffers can be treacherous territory.

If money was one reason you were unhappy in your current job, presumably you asked your boss for a raise and were denied it before you went looking for a new job. You should question why the company now is suddenly willing to give you that raise.

Yes, it's possible that your boss just wasn't paying attention to market salaries and wasn't aware that a raise was appropriate. It's also possible that your boss simply needs to keep you around long enough for the company to find a replacement and plans to drop you like a hot potato as soon as someone else is hired. At the very least, your boss may resent your seeking offers elsewhere and forcing the company to give you more money, and those feelings may damage your working relationship. So before you accept your boss's counteroffer, make sure that you won't be treated as persona non grata—or fired within a few months—because of your perceived disloyalty.

Asking the new employer for more money based on the counteroffer poses some danger as well. At worst, the company may withdraw its offer. Even if the new employer matches or beats the counteroffer, your working relationship is off to a less-than-ideal start. You did, after all, make a good-faith deal with the employer, and now you're going back on your word.

If you decide you can live with this risk, be extremely diplomatic and understanding when you approach the new employer. Apologize for having to reopen the salary issue and explain the situation by saying something like:

> *"I realize that we had a salary agreement, but something unexpected happened when I resigned. My current employer offered me $5,000 more than your company, and it's difficult for me to justify turning that offer down. Is there a possibility you can match it?"*

Don't back yourself into a corner by saying that you can't accept the new job if the employer can't match the counteroffer, unless you're sure you want to stay where you're at if the new employer won't up the ante. If you do decide to keep your old job, let the new employer know immediately. Follow up with a letter saying that you appreciate the company's interest and you regret any inconvenience your decision has caused. Similarly, if you decide to take the new job, be sure to send a polite memo informing your boss of your final decision and expressing your appreciation for the counteroffer.

Don't look back

Most people have a strange reaction after they accept a job offer. They're elated initially, but they soon start having second thoughts.

You'll probably experience the same doubts when you say yes to a new job. You may wonder whether you'll really like the work. You may question whether you should have asked for more money. You may be nervous about trying to fit in someplace new or taking on new challenges.

Understand that these feelings are entirely natural. After all, your life is about to change. But don't let fears of the unknown spoil your excitement or, worse, convince you to turn back. You've made an informed, carefully thought-out decision, so celebrate your success and forge ahead on your new adventure. The same strength, smarts and savvy that helped you emerge victorious from a very difficult job hunt will enable you to be just as successful on the job.

Chapter 19

Negotiating a raise

You've been on the job for a year, two years, perhaps even longer. You get a lot of satisfaction out of your work—except on payday. When you look at your pay stub, the number in the little box marked "wages, tips and other compensation" just isn't as big as it should be. You know you're underpaid, but your employer doesn't seem to agree. The raise you get with your annual performance review is minimal, and your requests for a larger salary increase fall on deaf ears.

If this describes your situation, it's possible that you need to make some changes in the way you approach the issue of getting a raise.

How the system works

Most companies today have a policy of reviewing employee salaries and performance on a regular basis. Usually, employees are reviewed three or six months after they're first hired and then once a year for the remainder of their employment.

Unless your company is suffering severe financial problems, you usually can expect some salary increase at the time of your review. Theoretically, the amount of your raise should depend on how well you're doing your job. I say "theoretically" because although some employers really do pay attention to performance when doling out raises, others give the same percentage to everyone, achievers and slackers alike. Although the percentage of annual increase varies from company to company and industry to industry, the average right now is about 3 to 5 percent.

Let's suppose that you accept your 3 to 5 percent graciously during your annual review but then decide after a few months that your compensation is not appropriate. Do you have to wait until your next review to ask for a raise? No, but your chances of getting your request approved aren't great because you're working outside the boundaries of the established salary review system.

As a rule, employers don't like to break from the system of increasing salaries at specified intervals because they plan their budgets around that system. If you ask for a raise between reviews, your boss probably will have to jump through a lot of hoops to get approval from higher-ups. Most bosses won't be willing to do that—and most companies won't be willing to approve the request—unless two conditions exist: a) you're invaluable to the department; and b) you announce that you're leaving if the company can't meet your terms.

Although threatening to quit may get your employer's attention, it can also backfire, so consider carefully before you use this tactic. If the company refuses your request, you're in a real bind; you'll never be taken seriously again if you don't carry out your threat. And if your boss does give in and raise your salary, your working relationship may be damaged. People don't like to be bullied or blackmailed into an agreement, especially bosses.

Telling your boss that someone else has made you a better offer is not always a good idea, either. If you've made up your mind that you will leave your present job if the company won't match the new employer's offer, go ahead and say so. Explain that you'd like to stay but you can't justify working for less than you can earn elsewhere. But if you're not really sure you do want to quit, you may want to be more discreet. You can say something like, "I've been looking into the marketplace and I've found that my skills are worth more." Otherwise, you put yourself in the position of having to quit to save face if your boss won't approve your raise. In addition, if the corporate culture is one that values company loyalty highly, your reputation in the organization may be hurt if word gets out that you're interviewing for other jobs.

The moral of the story is that you're better off to make your salary requests within the confines of the annual review. Even then, however, you'll have to work hard to convince your boss to give you anything over and above what the company has established as its average annual increase.

Each year at budget time, your department manager must set aside a certain amount for wages. To arrive at that budget figure, your manager totals up the salaries of everyone in the department and adds whatever percentage the company dictates is to be the annual increase that year. If you request more money than is allotted for you, your manager has to find cash elsewhere in the budget and get approval to shift the funds.

If you want to have any hope of getting more than the average salary increase at your review, you must convince your boss that you're valuable enough to make all of the necessary extra budget and approval footwork worthwhile. In order to do that, you must prepare very carefully for your review. You also must use all of the sales skills discussed earlier in this book when you present your request to your boss.

Justify your request

The first step to take when preparing for your review is to think about all of the reasons why a raise is justified. Unfortunately, "because I need more money" is not a good argument for a raise. Few employers will agree to give you more money just because you need it to pay your bills.

In order to justify your request, you must be able to answer "yes" to one or more of the following questions:

- Is your salary below market rate?
- Have you taken on additional responsibilities without any adjustment in compensation?
- Do you add more value to the company than co-workers earning the same salary?

Most employers do want to pay fair wages, if only because they don't want to get a reputation for being cheap. If you can offer evidence to support your claim that you're paid less than the going rate or that you're handling tasks outside of your existing job description, you have a better chance of getting the raise you want.

Your case is even stronger if you can prove that you did more than just sit at your desk and turn in an average performance. If you can't do that, the employer has little to risk by refusing your raise. It won't matter much to the employer if you get angry and quit, because you're not accomplishing anything that the next person on the street couldn't do.

Make your case in writing

Your second step is to prepare a short, one- or two-page document that lists the important goals you've achieved, projects you've completed and other on-the-job accomplishments since your last review. Creating a written account of your efforts is important because it helps your boss see in concrete terms why an increase is appropriate. If your boss must get higher-ups to approve your raise, this hard evidence also will help him or her make your case for you.

Describe in very specific terms how your efforts benefited the company—how you saved money, made money, increased customer satisfaction or otherwise improved things. If possible, compare your performance with that of others in your department and list those areas in which you excelled. For example, if you handled an average of 20 customer calls an hour, but the department average was 16 calls an hour, note that you exceeded the average by 25 percent. In addition, write down any new responsibilities you've assumed that were not included in your original job description.

If you're asking for a raise because your salary is below market rate, also provide written evidence of what other employers are paying. It will be harder for your employer to ignore claims of low wages when the proof is right there in black and white. Cite at least two or three credible sources of salary information—possibilities include trade organizations, business publications, the Department of Labor and college-placement offices.

(See Chapter 10 for more information on collecting salary data.) You also can conduct an informal survey by calling recruiting firms, clipping classified ads that state the salary range for positions similar to yours and talking to others in your field.

Lay the proper groundwork

Some companies pay strict attention to their performance review schedules, but others don't. If yours is of the latter type, you may have to push to get your review on time. It's not a favorite activity of most managers, so your boss may put it off forever if you don't ask. Just to be on the safe side, find time to have an informal chat with your boss a few weeks before your review date.

During your conversation, set an appointment for your review and give your boss a copy of the performance report you created. When you do this, you can say something like:

> *"In preparation for my review, I've jotted down a few thoughts about my performance during this last year. I'd especially like to get your feedback on these issues when we meet."*

It's also a good idea to give some advance notice of your dissatisfaction with your salary. You can do this by saying something to the effect of:

> *"I do want to let you know that I believe that my compensation is no longer where it should be. Based on the current market value of my skills and on my performance, my salary is off by about 12 percent."*

Giving advance notice that salary negotiation is pending prompts your boss to start thinking about how much value you add to the organization and how it would affect the department if you left. Laying this psychological groundwork increases the chances that your boss will agree that it's worth paying you more to keep you around.

Ask for more than you expect to get

At minimum, you should always strive to earn fair market value for your skills. However, to give yourself room for nego-tiation, ask for a little bit more of an increase than you think you can get. Then work downward toward a middle ground between your initial request and your boss's offer. This allows for a win-win negotiation. Each side gives some ground, but each side also leaves the negotiation feeling that they gained some ground.

Don't be too modest

In the typical performance review system, department managers must fill out generic evaluation forms that rate each employee's performance. Many times, managers ask employees to fill out self-evaluation forms as well. They do so because they believe that it's helpful to know how employees see themselves.

This practice poses some special pitfalls for women. Just as women tend to downplay their accomplishments during job interviews, they often aren't comfortable giving themselves good marks in their self-evaluations. Mike Matta, development director for the retained-search firm R.E. Lowe, tells a story that typifies this response. "I was talking with a woman whose boss asked her to fill out a self-evaluation form prior to a review," recalls Matta. "Based on what she told me about her skills and accomplishments, I recommended that she rank herself as superior in several categories and as excellent in others. Her response was, 'I can't turn in comments like that—I'd be praising myself too much.'"

Interestingly, several other men have told me the exact same story about female friends who underrated themselves in self-evaluations. In each case, the woman fully deserved superior performance marks but wasn't comfortable saying so.

If you feel this way, it's critical that you get over your fears, both when you fill out formal self-evaluations and when you prepare your own performance report prior to your review. Evaluate yourself as a mediocre performer, and you give your boss ample reason to award you a mediocre raise.

If you are truly superior in a certain performance category, give yourself a superior rating. When the form allows, note an accomplishment that supports your evaluation of your skills. If you believe you need work in a certain area, it's okay to give yourself lesser marks, but be sure to note what actions you're taking to improve those skills.

After you complete your self-evaluation, you may want to show it to a trusted co-worker and ask whether your perceptions of yourself are on target. If anything, you should be a little more generous with your evaluations than you think others might be. After all, if you're not in your corner, no one else is likely to make a stand for you either.

Speak up if you don't agree

During your review, if you disagree with your manager's evaluation of you, don't just let the issue slide. Without sounding defensive or angry, ask your boss to explain why your performance was lacking. Request solid evidence of why you weren't given the marks you think you deserve. Many times, these performance rankings are subjective, and if you can provide evidence demonstrating that the review is off-base, you may be able to persuade your boss to upgrade your evaluation.

When your boss announces the amount of your raise, be sure to ask how that amount compares with the average increase being awarded. If you're on the low end of the scale, ask why. Then, if the raise does not meet your satisfaction, it's time to open negotiations.

Again, don't act indignant over the amount of the raise. Calmly say that you appreciate the fact that your boss sees fit to increase your pay, but you believe a higher amount is appropriate. State the figure you want and explain why that compensation is fair. Then negotiate your raise using the strategies laid out in the last two chapters and in the rest of this chapter.

Set goals for next year

In addition to being the best time to negotiate compensation for your performance over the past year, your annual review is the best time to build a framework for a raise at next year's review. Before leaving your review, talk with your boss about how you can increase your value to the company even further. Express your interest in taking on challenges or participating in important projects.

It's also a good idea to draw up a list of performance goals that you will try to accomplish during the next 12 months and to suggest appropriate rewards for meeting those goals. Set reasonable goals; you don't want to come to your next review without accomplishing anything you said you could do. Follow up your meeting with a memo that puts any agreement about goals and rewards in writing, because this document will strengthen your position at your next review.

Raises between reviews

As you learned earlier, your chances of getting a raise between reviews aren't terribly good if you work for an employer that follows a strict performance-review schedule. However, providing that you approach the subject professionally, it never hurts to try to improve your compensation if you're dissatisfied. It's a sure bet you won't get what you want if you don't ask.

Approach this request for a raise just as you would your performance review. In writing, document the reasons why the raise is in order and then ask your boss for a meeting to discuss compensation. When you ask for the meeting, provide your boss with a copy of your written documentation and give some indication of how much of an increase you're seeking. During your meeting, negotiate your raise just as you would during an annual review.

For raises between reviews, the timing of your request is especially important. Obviously, you don't want to initiate conversations about a raise when your boss is clearly having a bad day or is trying to meet some important deadline. Wait until the boss is in a more positive and relaxed mood.

The best time to ask for a raise is when you've just accomplished some major goal—hopefully, one that made a major impact on the company. Your bargaining power is always greater when your contributions are fresh in everyone's mind.

It helps, too, to put yourself in the spotlight as much as possible in the months before you ask for a raise. For example, send a memo to your superiors to announce that you've accomplished a major goal—and include data to show how the company's bottom line has been improved as a result. If you've completed an important project recently, schedule a presentation to explain the project to management. In other words, do some self-promotion to remind management who you are and what you can do. You may be keeping such a low profile that the powers that be may not realize how much you're doing for the company.

Attitude counts

Whether you're asking for a raise in conjunction with your annual review or between reviews, it's important to maintain the right attitude when you negotiate a raise. Be firm in your request, but also be polite and professional. Approach your boss with a positive attitude rather than a negative one. As the saying goes, you catch more flies with honey than with vinegar.

Suppose, for example, that you're asking for a raise because you've determined that the company is paying below market value. Instead of accusing the company of deliberately paying low wages, help your boss understand how the current pay scale may be hurting the company. It's very possible that the employer simply isn't aware that salaries are out of line. You can alert your boss to the problem by saying something like:

> *"It occurred to me that you may not be aware of how our company's compensation stacks up in the marketplace. Here's some evidence I've gathered about what other employers are paying. As you can see, our salary scale isn't up to par. I think you need to know, because it may cause us to lose some good people."*

Similarly, if your boss turns down your request initially, don't get angry or defensive; it won't help you achieve your goal. Instead, ask how you can increase your value to the company. Suggest that you assume additional tasks in exchange for the salary increase, for example, or establish some specific goals and rewards that will enable you to reach your desired compensation level.

As you do in salary negotiations when you're taking a new job, let your boss know that you're interested in a win-win solution. Explain that an increase in salary will not only enable you to renew your commitment to the company, but also will motivate you to work even harder to help your department succeed and to help the company prosper. You want to send the message, "If you and I can agree on this, we both win."

Overcoming objections

It's not likely that your boss will agree to your request in total without any argument at all. Remember, every dollar your boss gives you is a dollar that must be accounted for in the department's budget, and managers are rewarded for keeping budget expenditures small.

Because denying an employee a raise is an awkward situation—nobody likes to be the bad guy—managers sometimes fall back on excuses that remove the blame from their shoulders. Instead of saying, "You haven't convinced me that you're worth that much," for example, they'll say, "We don't have any more money in our budget." When you hear such excuses, you know you need to go back and restate your accomplishments and your value to the company. In other words, you need to do more to help your boss see how the company will benefit by giving you the raise.

In some cases, of course, there really isn't any more money, or some other condition exists that prevents your boss from giving you the raise. Even so, that doesn't mean the issue of higher compensation is dead in the water. You simply need to be a bit more creative in your negotiating.

Here's a closer look at some of the more common excuses employers use when denying raises, along with suggestions on how to work your way past these objections.

1. "We're in a salary freeze right now."

If the company has established a formal salary freeze, find out when it will end. But don't wait until that date to negotiate your raise. Instead, try to get your boss to agree to a certain salary increase now, with the understanding that it will take effect immediately after the salary freeze is lifted. When that freeze is removed, there will be a lot of people asking for more money. You want to be the first one in line.

Also consider negotiating for non-cash benefits instead of an actual wage increase. For example, ask to be assigned to a plum project that will give you valuable experience or put you in line for a promotion, or ask for more flexible hours or extra vacation days in lieu of a raise.

2. "You're at the top of your salary grade."

In most companies that use a salary-grade structure, your boss won't be able to give you more than the highest salary in the range. To work around this, you can do one of two things. One option is to focus on getting a promotion to a job that falls in a higher pay-grade level. Ask your boss what you need to do to move up, and then work toward that goal. In the meantime, negotiate for added non-cash benefits to increase your compensation for doing your current job. One-time bonus payments may also be possible.

Second, you can ask that your job title be revised so that you then can be reassigned to a higher salary-grade level. This will be easier for your boss to do if you've taken on additional responsibilities outside of your original job description. When you request this change in title, however, understand that you're asking your boss to make a special effort on your behalf. Be sure to tell your boss that you appreciate this effort, and offer to do anything you can to make the process easier.

3. "Our budget is very limited right now."

To counter this objection, remind your boss of contributions that made a positive impact on the budget. For example:

> "Yes, I know that things are tight now. However, I'd like to remind you that because of my negotiations with our ad agency, I reduced our expenses by $40,000 last year. That project alone will pay for my $4,000 raise and leave you $36,000 more in your annual budget."

Let's suppose that there really isn't a spare dime to be found in the company compensation budget—not a rare case in this day and age. If you determine that your employer really can't afford to pay you more, set up a schedule of goals and rewards for the future. Look around for problems that are costing the department money. Then ask your boss to agree that if you solve those problems, you'll be awarded a bonus or salary increase based on the amount of money you save the company.

4. "You'd be earning more than others at that level."

Many employers prefer to pay everyone who has the same job title the same amount of money, because it helps eliminate dissension among the ranks. Fortunately, the trend toward performance-based pay—in which employees are paid based on their individual contributions—is coming back into vogue. If your company hasn't jumped on this very sensible bandwagon yet, perhaps you can help push it on board. Point out those areas in which you are contributing more than others in the department and suggest that you are therefore deserving of more compensation.

If you can't sell your boss on the notion that you should be paid additional money because you're worth more to the company, try focusing on the additional duties you've assumed. Request that your title be changed to reflect those additional responsibilities. Once you no longer have the same job title as everyone else, the argument that you can't make more money than everyone else disappears.

Promote yourself

One of the fastest ways to make substantial salary gains, of course, is to get a promotion to a higher-level job. And the best way to put yourself in the running for a promotion is to lobby actively for it.

Many women neglect this very important aspect of their careers. They're either too shy to say they want a promotion, or they believe that it's not necessary to do so. They expect that if they do a good job, they'll automatically get the recognition and promotions they deserve. The business world, unfortunately, does not work this way.

Take the sit-and-wait approach, and you'll be sitting and waiting a long time. If you don't make your feelings known, your boss will assume that you're happy where you are. While you wait for someone to ask you to interview for the promotion, your male colleagues and more proactive female co-workers are forging ahead, selling themselves as the perfect people for the job.

When you hear of an opening that interests you or believe you're ready to advance, update your resume, hand it to your boss or the appropriate hiring manager, and ask for an appointment to discuss the subject. Remember that in business, the old adage, "All good things come to those who wait" does not apply.

Beware promotions without pay

Lately, I've been hearing more and more stories about employers who ask staff members to assume a higher level of responsibility without any additional compensation. Often, these "promotions" are presented as a chance to be "acting manager" or "acting director" of the department. That means that you do the work of the director or the manager without the official title or salary until such time as the employer makes a firm decision about giving you the job permanently.

It's true that such situations do give you an opportunity to prove that you're ready for promotion. The problem is that these temporary arrangements have a tendency to drag on longer than they should. Although you should seize the chance to assume more responsibility if that is your career goal, be sure to establish some ground rules before you accept a promotion without appropriate compensation.

Ask when you will be eligible to assume the official title and accompanying salary if you take the job. Also ask what goals you'll have to meet to be given the job permanently. Then get all of those details in writing. When your trial period is nearly finished, prepare a report of your accomplishments and set up a meeting with your boss to discuss your permanent promotion.

Don't relax after you get the raise

After you celebrate your raise or promotion, you can't afford to rest on your laurels. If you want to keep moving forward in your career, you must continue marketing yourself to your boss and to others in the company. In addition, you must always keep your eye on the market value of your skills. Remember that it's up to you to make sure that you're getting a fair price for your services.

Chapter 20

When you need help

Today's business world can be an exciting, rewarding place for a woman. It also can be full of frustration, disappointment and rejection.

There will be times in your job search and in your career when things seem terribly discouraging. You interview for several jobs and get no offers. You ask for a raise and are turned down cold. You turn in a stellar performance year after year but can't make even a small chip in your employer's glass ceiling.

At such times, it's easy to lose faith in yourself, to stop trying. But if you give in to these feelings, you compound your problems. When you're depressed and discouraged, it's doubly difficult to sell yourself to an employer or to accomplish your goals on the job. So instead of pummeling yourself with thoughts of failure and defeat, turn that negative energy into positive action.

If your interviews aren't going as well as you'd like, do some more role-playing with a friend to refine your presentation. If your employer refuses to pay you what you're worth or continues to discriminate against women, don't just sit there hoping things will improve—start looking for a better job. Call up your networking contacts, get in touch with a recruiter and arrange some information interviews. There are many employers who would be more than happy to have your services and to treat you fairly; make it your business to find them.

In addition, seek out and take advantage of the many career support resources available to you. The list here provides information on just a few of the many organizations and agencies that can help you improve your interviewing skills, provide you with job training and counsel you on how to handle employment discrimination. You should be able to find many other resources in your neighborhood by calling the placement office of your local community college, looking in the yellow pages under "Career and Vocational Counseling," and checking your newspaper or library bulletin board for notices of upcoming career seminars and job-training programs.

When things look bleak, step back and analyze your problems from an objective viewpoint. Then plot a specific course of action and commit yourself to taking at least one step each day toward getting your career back on track. Remember, a smart woman does not sit and wait for opportunity to knock on her door—she goes out in search of it.

Organizations offering career support

Forty Plus of New York
15 Park Row
New York, NY 10038
212-233-6086
Fax: 212-227-2974

The 21 Forty Plus organizations across the country, each operating independently, offer help to out-of-work women and men over 40 who have previously been employed in management or in a professional occupation. Membership includes a comprehensive job-hunt campaign package, consisting of career counseling, assistance with resume-writing, networking tips, interviewing skills and more. Members have access to Forty Plus facilities, which include word processing, computer and office support. Best of all, members can count on the expertise, advice and support of their peers. Membership fees vary for each organization. Call Forty Plus of New York for information on the center nearest you.

National Displaced Homemakers Network
1625 K Street NW, Suite 300
Washington, D.C. 20006
202-467-6346

This grant-funded program supports 1,100 regional programs that offer individual career counseling as well as workshops on career planning, job hunting and self-esteem.
Membership is $15 and includes a newsletter "Network News,"
mailed four times a year, which features occupational information and more. Call for the center nearest you.

9to5, National Association of Working Women
238 W. Wisconsin Ave., Suite 700
Milwaukee, WI 53203
414-274-0925

This well-known membership organization lobbies actively
in support of legislation that protects the rights of working
women. In addition, it offers a broad range of publications on
topics such as sexual harassment, family leave and office
health and safety. Women needing advice about sexual harassment, job discrimination or other workplace issues can call
9to5's toll-free job problems hotline, 800-522-0925. The current
membership fee is $25, for which you receive the 9to5 newslet-
ter, published five times a year; discounts on other 9to5 publications; and a variety of other benefits.

Women's Wire
1820 Gateway Dr.
San Mateo, CA 94404
415-378-6500

This commercial online service provides information about
topics of interest to women, from spousal abuse to women's
health issues to job and career concerns. Members can communicate via e-mail, open forums, private chats and scheduled
conferences. There's a monthly service charge of $9.95.

U.S. Department of Labor, Women's Bureau
200 Constitution Ave., NW
Washington, D.C. 20210
202-219-6593

The Women's Bureau, which has regional offices across the country, offers many informative publications—almost all of which are free. Among those that every woman should read are "A Working Woman's Guide to Her Job Rights," a 72-page booklet that explains in detail the laws that protect you on the job and the steps you should take if your rights are violated. Another great resource is the *Directory of Nontraditional Training and Employment Programs Serving Women*, a 157-page guide to programs that assist women in obtaining training and employment in fields traditionally dominated by men, such as plumbing, diesel mechanics and drafting. For a publications order form or for the address of the regional office nearest you, call or write the Washington headquarters.

U.S. Government Employment Training Programs

The government, through the Job Training Partnership Act and a variety of federally funded projects, provides many valuable career-support services, including job-search assistance, training in interviewing skills and resume-writing workshops. For information on available programs in your area, call your state department of labor or human resources.

A

B

C

H

Hassinger, Jane, 28-29, 32, 34, 96
Human resources
  department (HR), 58, 174

I

Impression, first, 79-80, 83-90
Information interviews, 39-47
Insecurity, 32-33
Insurance, 188
Interview
  all-day, 149
  appearance for, 80, 83-85, 161
  behavioral, 56, 109, 118
  campus recruiting, 147-148
  committee, 151
  computer, 60-61
  consensus, 58-59
  conversational, 57
  etiquette for, 79, 87-89
  fear of, 49-53
  follow-up to, 165-171
  information, 39-47
  out-of-town, 148-149
  practicing for, 74
  questions during, 45, 113-132
  rehearsing for, 159-164
  research for, 99-112
  restaurant, 149-150
  special situations, 145-158
  stress, 151
  team, 58-59
  telephone, 152-153
  with recruiters, 153-154
Interviewer
  "non-," 156-157
  hostile, 155-156

romantic, 154-155
inexperienced, 51-52
Interviewing styles, 55-62
Interviewing the
  employer, 133-144
Inventory, skills, 105-107

J

Job offer, responding to,
  186-195
Job Training Partnership
  Act, 216
Job-hopping, questions
  about, 128

K

Koons, Stephanie, 32
Kornhauser, David, 56, 59

L

Lane, Darla, 30, 34-35
Language patterns, 92-94
Language, body, 78, 80,
  85-87, 143, 161, 179
Layoff, questions
  about, 128-129
Letter, thank-you, 166-169
Library research, 101
Listening skills, 36, 72-73

M

Makeup, for an interview, 84
Management, team-based, 36
Matta, Mike, 96, 204

Modesty, 27-30
Moving expenses, 188

N

National Displaced
  Homemakers Network, 215
Needs, focusing on, 65-66
Negotiating a raise, 199-212
Negotiation, salary, 33-34,
  129-131, 173-198
Networking, 40-41, 101-103
9to5, National Association of
  Working Women, 25, 215
"Non-interviewer," 156-157
Notice to old employer, 196

O

Objections
  anticipating, 69-71, 110-111
  to raise requests, 208-210
Objective, career, 42-43
Olson, Cheryl, 28-29
Open-ended questions, 115-116
Out-of-town interviews,
  148-149
Overtime policies, 188

P

Pension plans, 188
Personal relationship with
  employer, 40-41
Personality
  questions about, 119-125
  test, 59
"Playing fair," 35-36
Post-Interview Syndrome, 165

Practicing for an
  interview, 74
Problem-solving, 64-74
Profit-sharing plans, 188
Profitability, company, 67
Promoting yourself, 210-211
Promotions without pay, 211
Proving your value, 66-68
Psychological profile, 59
Punctuality for an
  interview, 87-88

Q

Qualifications,
  ranking your, 107-108
Qualities sought by
  employers, 61-62
Questions, interview, 45, 73,
  113-144

R

Raise, negotiating a, 199-212
Rapport, establishing, 74-82
Recruiters, 102, 153-154, 175
References, 111-112
Rehearsing for interviews,
  159-164
Rejection, 171
Relaxation strategies, 163
Researching
  companies, 40, 45, 64-65, 99-102
  contacts, 43-44
  positions, 102-103
  salaries, 103-104
Resources, support, 213-216
Restaurant interview, 149-150
Rettig-Drufke, Susan, 17, 21, 97